I0477010

0 TO 6 FIGURES AND BEYOND:

Uncover the Secrets to the WealthPreneur Strategy:

(Entrepreneurs Express Lanes)

Ruddy Palacios

0 TO 6 FIGURES AND BEYOND:

UNCOVER THE SECRETS TO THE WEALTHPRENEUR STRATEGY

Copyright 2015 by Ruddy Palacios

All rights reserved.

No part of this book may be reproduced in any form or by any electronic or mechanical means, including information storage and retrieval systems, without permission in writing from the publisher. The only exception is by a reviewer, who may quote short excerpts in a published review.

Published by: CreateSpace Inc.

ISBN PAPERBACK: 978-1523308262 Library of Congress Control Number: 1523308265

Cover design by Ruddy Palacios and Associates Interior design Create Space Printed in the USA

The information presented herein represents the view of the author as of the date of publication. This book is presented for informational purposes only. Due to the rate at which conditions change, the author reserves the right to alter and update his opinions based on new conditions. While every attempt has been made to verify the information in this book, neither the author nor his affiliates/partners assume any responsibility for errors, inaccuracies, or omissions.

Connect With Us

To Purchase:

0 To 6 Figures And Beyond can be purchased via the following venues:

Paperback:

Publisher: Create Space

Amazon.com: Get 0 To 6 Figures And Beyond on Amazon

EBook:

On your iPad or iPhone via Apple's iBooks

On your Kindle or your B&N Nook

To Connect:

www.facebook.com/wealthpreneurs.tm

www.thewealthstrategy.com

www.RuddyPalacios.com

www.twitter.com/wealth_preneur

www.instagram.com/0to6figuresclub

Dedication

A Mi Madre Bella:

Gracias por ser una gran y amorosa madre. Gracias por todos los sacrificios que as hecho por mi. Gracias por ser tan buen ser humano y siempre creer en mi. Gracias porque siempre me has dicho que yo fui echo para ser cosas grandes, Te amo !

To My Wife and Kids:

Jen, thank you for loving me, supporting my goals, and being with me from the start, through my many failures and few successes. Thank you for being so great at everything I am not. I would not be able to do everything I do without you, or eat the delicious all-organic, nutritious food you so lovingly make for my kids and me. Zayden, my firstborn son, you light up every single day with that marvelous, captivating smile; you motivate me to do more and be more. My daughter, who is due about three months from today and will probably be born by the time this book is published, the thought of you has ignited a fire in my consciousness like nothing ever felt before; you are and will be very loved.

To All of My Students:

I am so grateful for each and every one of you; your successes and amazing testimonials have allowed me to live a life of tremendous significance, purpose, and human connection.

CONTENTS

PREFACE

THE "WHY" BEHIND ZERO TO 6 FIGURES AND BEYOND

The inspiration behind this book dates back to the beginning of my career as a mentor and entrepreneur coach. I got the same feedback from my first three one-on-one consultations with students: "WOW, a real FAST-TRACK system." All three of those students were amazed with my system and the unconventional information I was openly sharing with them. They, like all the students who came after them, were fascinated with the life-changing information. Two of my first three students were young college grads with master's degrees in business from reputable schools like UCLA and Cal State Fullerton. The other student was in the military for the last decade of his life, serving our country. All three of them were in "AWH" after their one-on-ones because all their lives they had been taught conventional ways to make money that did not work.

They each told me almost verbatim, "Ruddy, I really thought I had to work hard all my life, save money from every paycheck, invest in my 401k, buy a home as quickly as possible, and hopefully retire in forty years. I had no idea there was any other way to do it. That is how my parents did it, and in school they didn't tell us any different, so I assumed that is how things were. I did not like it, which is why I searched for better ways, which led me to you." When I shared my system, they realized the truth behind these conventional ways; they understood that these old methods made absolutely no sense and would only lead them down a path of mediocrity.

The low- and middle-class population has been conditioned to believe the old methods being taught by the mainstream: the good ol' "work hard, go to college, hope to get a good job, save 10% of your post-tax income, invest in a 401k, and hopefully have enough to retire in your sixties." Well, if you look at the cold, hard numbers and stats of retirees, you will quickly find out that this is a path that will handcuff you to work for the rest of your life and most likely live paycheck to paycheck until the day you die. The truth is, this old "industrial" system no longer works. I shared with my students the truth: men lie, women lie, numbers don't.

The numbers from the abstract published by the Bureau of the Census and researchscape.com clearly show that only 10% of the men in America over the age of sixty-five have incomes of over 6K per month; over 80% have incomes of less than 4K per month. We are in the information age; anyone who wants to thrive in this age and economy needs to know the rules so that they can evolve and adapt to a system that works today!

Those three students, like hundreds of students who came after them, got on the FasTrak, speeding down the track toward financial freedom. The repeated feedback from everyone was that I needed to write a book in order to help more people since I do not have the time to coach millions. Putting my system and knowledge into a book would allow those who seek wealth to find a true, honest mechanism that works!

They wanted to have something easy and tangible to give to their friends, family, and clients they cared about. So after years of requests, I finally sat my butt down to put my system into a book form, up for grabs, for the world to have a cutting-edge financial education that, if used ethically and implemented correctly, can quickly change the quality of your life and the course of not only your but your whole family's future.

INTRODUCTION

I am here to share with you some great news: There is a proven system and path to help you retire in a rapid seven to ten years depending on how committed you are and how well you implement the mechanisms I will teach you in this book. The track I am going to take you down will allow you to bypass years of grief and modern-day slavery to the industrial age that most people are living in. The methodology still being taught today by conventional education, the school system, the media, and governments will lead you down a path of inferiority and having to work hard all your life building someone else's dream. People like myself and others have defied conventional methods and have decoded the cipher to live a dream life and to have financial freedom on a "FasTrak."

The current system the masses are adhering to makes me sick to my stomach. I cannot believe a system that creates modern-day slavery is still so mainstream; this ideology is heavily taught and programmed into the majority of society. The old industrial-age tale is told as follows: Go to school (where they train you to be a good employee), get good grades (which programs you to be a linear thinker), get a good job (which means to become someone's slave for pay), invest in the stock market and max out your 401k (which is basically gambling with your slave-earned money, playing a game you don't know the rules to), buy a house (which is not an asset and in most cases is a liability), retire in your sixties and hope you have enough savings and Social Security income to enjoy your retirement. (In your sixties? What happened to enjoying your life from twenty to sixty? That is forty years of your short-lived human existence gone, doing what?)

The reality is that over 95% of the world lives enslaved all their lives via this huge lie that in their sixties things will be better. The truth is that it typically only gets worse. According to the Employee Benefit Research Institute (ebri.org), the majority of people fifty-five years and older live 100% below poverty-level income, and the majority of people seventy-five years and older live 200% below the poverty level—that is, if you're lucky and healthy enough to live that long. That is not and will not be the reality for my students, and now the millions of people who will read this life-transforming book. With the help of the FasTrak, those who have the will to alter their lives, WILL.

"Whether you think you CAN or CAN'T, you are right." – Henry Ford. **The information in this book will work only for those willing to put in the work and take massive action. People always say, "Do it like your life depended on it." Well, guess what. Your life does depend on it. Again, this will work only for people willing and wanting to improve their quality of life. The truth is that not everyone wants to change their life for the better, and that is okay, but I am 100% confident that anyone truly WILLING, CAN. This book, along with your focus and action, will give you the tools, systems, and mechanisms to transform your life.**

The WealthPreneur Strategy is the vehicle that will allow you to avoid all the traffic and red lights that society currently has in place. This delayed way of doing things is like taking the "bus to wealth." The FasTrak is a system that will allow you to quickly learn, live, and teach mechanisms of the WEALTHY.

You see, becoming wealthy is an art I will be teaching you: the craft to creating wealth, which I have learned from some of the most successful humans who ever stepped on our planet. After learning these mechanisms, I was able to start living them and manifesting them in my own life, and now I am able to teach them to everyone and anyone willing to learn.

The WealthPreneur Strategy will involve rewiring your mental thinking (your mindset) into a state of confidence that will create a happy, prosperous, healthy, and wealthy individual with amazing relationships with every person he or she comes across.

These systems will allow you to learn how to start your own corporation, understand how to raise capital and obtain hundreds of thousands of dollars in business credit from banks and other financial institutions. You need to learn how to raise capital before you even have a business because once you have capital, then you can really go into any business you are passionate about.

After you come up with a business you are passionate about, you need to understand how to market that business efficiently online and offline. One of the most powerful techniques in the modern information age in which we are currently living is "inbound marketing." Once you have successful marketing techniques that can be applied to any business, you need to learn how to close your leads effectively. With that in mind, you need strong sales skills that work ethically and dynamically.

When you are closing sales profitably, you are making money and moving closer to becoming financially free. Once your business is bringing in substantial income and you have hundreds of thousands—

and, subsequently, millions—of dollars coming in from your well-functioning business system, you need to learn how to invest this money wisely and affluently. Do you go into real estate? The stock market? Other businesses? We will get into those details in later chapters.

One of the last steps in the FasTrak strategy is to learn how to automate your business and implement all the formulas that the wealthy utilize to their advantage. This is so that you stop trading time for money (modern-day slavery) and simply trade money for money or trade very little time for huge amounts of money.

This is called leveraging your money and, most importantly, your time. Time is priceless. I am sure you have heard the saying, "You can always get more money, but you cannot get more time." This is a very true statement because we have only twenty-four hours in a day. However, the amount of money we can make in a day is unlimited depending on one's money thermometer. Everyone has a money thermometer; it is basically the amount of money your subconscious believes you can make. Some people's thermometer is 50k per year; others' is six figures, and a very few have a money thermometer in the millions.

We will touch base in the first part of this book on how we can move up our money thermometers. Once your business is thriving and your investments are well-leveraged, which means that your money is producing more money through interest, you can start living the life of your dreams and having the financial freedom each and every human being alive deserves to live.

The phenomenal part of all this is that any willing being can accomplish it, realistically in seven to ten years of smart work, serious focus, and FasTrak education. Some people can and will accomplish their goal faster than others depending on variables like the number of hours spent following the FasTrak per day, natural-born talents, choosing good mentors, etc.

The part I am so fond of is that every willing soul who decides to drive their life through this FasTrak daily for seven to ten years will achieve financial freedom. They won't be taking the "bus to wealth," which involves working for the rest of their lives trading time for money and being shackled as prisoners to a nine-to-five job for forty years of their lives, hoping they can retire and enjoy the little bit of life they have left. The beautiful thing about the FasTrak strategy is that anyone who drives their life down this track will be financially free. There is no competition because there aren't enough people on the FasTrak, so anyone on it will get to their destination, which is wealth. Some will get to it faster than others depending on how fast they drive.

For those brave enough to choose the FasTrak, you will be able to do what you want, when you want, with the people you love most. There is so little traffic and competition on the FasTrak because only a very few are willing to pay the "toll fee." The "toll fee" is seven to ten years of not only hard work but smart work, long hours of being a producer, creative thinking, and calculated risk with massive amounts of FasTrak education in the aspects I discussed above.

You need to bring something to the marketplace that is different and a helpful solution to a problem. Your reward will be in exact proportion to the number of people you positively affect and help.

The FasTrak will teach you to **PROGRAM** the "Wealth Mindset" (1-percenter thinking), learning to reprogram your thought process, living your new thought process and mastering it so well that you can teach others. You will learn to **POSITION** yourself and your business to raise capital, to incorporate and structure the foundation of your business to make it easy to raise money from investors as well as obtain corporate and commercial business credit from financial institutions.

Move number three is **PROMOTING** and marketing your business **online and offline**. You'll be learning to develop effective inbound marketing systems that drive traffic and quality leads to your business sales funnel, leads that want what you have to sell and know that you are the only logical option. Next, through **PERSUASION** you'll be learning seven of the most effective closing techniques that work ethically and effectively. Last but not least, I will enable you to master passive income-investing vehicles that will allow you to **PROSPER**. You'll understand the most powerful ways of making your money work for you, instead of you working for your money. You'll be prevailing in the art of leveraging. Learning the concepts and strategies to create multiple passive income streams and applying them to your life will allow you to retire in seven to ten years. Those are the five P's of the WealthPreneur Strategy.

Wealth and retirement have different meanings to different people. What my FasTrak defines as wealth and retirement is having enough passive income to support the lifestyle you want to live without ever having to work again. By work I mean trading your time for money. For some people, depending on where you live in the world, wealth and retirement can be achieved by making only 8,500 USD, which is six figures a year passively without them having to trade time for money.

For others, this amount may be less. For individuals like myself, it takes a lot more because of the type of lifestyle I live. When you put the FasTrak system into action, the amount of income you can make actively and passively is limited only by your goal and the level of wealth you want to achieve.

This book will reveal everything you need to know to reach the level of wealth and success you seek. What I have noticed from the hundreds of wealth and personal development books I have read is that each book focuses only on one subject or one aspect of becoming wealthy.

Some of them touch on how to think positively or how to market your business or how to perform only one aspect of the wealth cipher. As good and helpful as those books may be, the fact is that a lot of them will leave you motivated with no real plan of action to put into place, no playbook that gives you a strong blueprint to drive you down a FasTrak to wealth.

Allow me to tell you a bit about the chief commander who will be conducting you through the FasTrak strategy for the next few hours. I am originally from Central America, the Costa Rica/Nicaragua region. My mother was forced to leave Costa Rica, fleeing my abusive father when I was three years old. She left my brother and me with my grandparents.

Since my biological father was an alcoholic and a drug abuser, my mother left seeking a better future for my brother and me. She fled to California with the plan to raise enough money and get legalized in the U.S., then come back for us. I did not have a mother or father for the first few years of my life, but I had amazing grandparents who took care of me.

My mother achieved her goal four years later and arranged to get my brother and me into the country and to become U.S. residents. I came to the U.S. when I was eight years old. I grew up in some rough parts of the California cities neighboring Compton and Long Beach.

Since I can remember, my family always lived paycheck to paycheck, struggling to make ends meet. We lived in some low- to middle-class neighborhoods where gang-banging, drug dealing, and crime were very common. My mom worked extremely hard but was always broke. As a kid I never understood why we struggled when my mom was always working and had very little time. Growing up, I was programmed with all the negative "enslaved route" thoughts that low- and middle-class people have, like "money doesn't come easy," "you have to work hard, go to college, find a good job," etc. My mom always worked for wealthy people, so I knew that there was a better way of doing things than what my family was doing.

At the age of sixteen I went into sales while still in high school because I had a strong entrepreneurial desire, and I was hungry to have a better quality of life. I really wanted to help my mom so that she could stop working so hard for people who did not appreciate her. I began reading every inspirational book and audio book I could get my hands on. I went through about a book a week in personal development and motivational material.

I did end up listening to my mom to satisfy her plea for me to attend college. I went to college, but after my first semester I dropped out. One of the many reasons was because I realized that, working part-time as a sales consultant at a law firm for attorneys nationwide, I was making more than my teachers did.

I saw how the founder of the company lived and went about running a successful business. There were a lot of multi-millionaires and former multi-millionaires who had lost millions when the economy crashed. There was a lot of talent that worked with me.

I was only eighteen years old, so I picked these people's brains daily and continued to do a lot of reading. I began figuring out what makes the haves and the have-nots. I began unlocking the secret to the FasTrak to wealth.

I became the number-one sales professional in that company of more than 500 employees—not number two or three, but number one—and the highest-paid consultant at the age of nineteen. I made well over six figures in 2009, which was considered one of the toughest years our economy had seen in a very long time. Since 2009 I have been able to increase my income each and every year and, most importantly, my assets, which equal my net worth. I started a few different businesses, incorporated sound corporate entities, and effectively invested my active six-figure income into phenomenal real estate assets for passive income. I became a mortgage broker and learned the art of leverage, lending out my own money as well as other people's money for an amazing passive return.

I invested in hard assets like gold and silver. I now own apartments in the U.S. and Central America. I quickly gained an abundance of knowledge and experience because I worked far more hours than the average person did in a short period of time. I also read two or three books a week and learned from extraordinary mentors.

The passive income I created from my assets allowed me to start mentoring students. I coached individuals of all ages and from all walks of life. They had different goals and different talents, but all had something in common—they were passionate and willing to take action to acquire financial freedom. Leading others down the FasTrak route and guiding them to financial freedom is one of the most rewarding responsibilities I have taken on.

I am now about sixty days away from turning twenty-five years old and have a net worth nearing seven figures along with multiple streams of income. I have an amazing wife, a son, and a daughter on the way (who will be born by the time this book is published). I live an amazing life in a beautiful home with my family in sunny Orange County, California. We drive luxury cars, travel wherever we want, and eat nothing but the highest-quality organic food that Whole Foods has to offer. I love wearing custom suits, playing soccer, strolling the Newport Beach boardwalk with my son, barbecuing with friends, and drinking quality wine by the fire pit in my backyard while writing down ideas about improving the quality of service businesses provide.

Whether people like me, dislike me, or even hate me, one thing they will all agree on is that my system to create wealth is effective and transformational. One thing I am is effective, and I have a track record for consistency and always delivering! So regardless of what you may think about me or my personal life, regardless of any positive or negative opinions you may hear from other people or the media, one thing is for certain: This book will have a significant impact on your life. All you have to do is read it and take action on its mechanisms. When you apply the information, you will achieve the level of success you desire and create the life you and your family deserve.

Everything I have learned that has made me successful up to this point is in this book. I will not hold back anything and will gift you the system that has unlocked the wealth cipher.

Almost every chapter will have specific action steps you must put into action to start achieving results and getting closer to your goal. So grab a notepad, sit somewhere comfortable, get some sort of caffeine in your system, and let's jump on the FasTrak to wealth.

PART 1

Programming the New Mind

CHAPTER 1-LIMITING AND ENSLAVED BELIEFS

Warning! The chapter you are about to read may puzzle you. It is indeed powerful. When you actually sit down and really THINK, you realize that a lot of this information is common sense, but sadly, common sense is not that common these days. When you really put this message into perspective, it is very logical.

The reason the "hoi polloi"—better-known as the general public or the common person—are not as wealthy and successful as they want to be because of the way they habitually think. The way the majority of people think about money, wealth, health, and happiness is flawed. The common person has erroneous limiting beliefs engrained and programmed into their subconscious mind. These beliefs are like a terminal disease that will keep you down the rest of your life if you don't take massive action to cure it.

The reason every person is in the situation they are in, good or bad, with a few notable exceptions, is because of the quality of thoughts they continually run through their mind. These thoughts form their current belief system. Most of the habitual thoughts an individual has in their life are programmed lessons taught by their parents, family, and teachers, as well as by the community they grew up in.

A lot of these limiting beliefs are created by the conversations you consciously and sub-consciously heard and witnessed as a child. Most low- and middle-class parents have negative thoughts about money; these thoughts were passed down by their parents.

These faulty and unsound thoughts about money, wealth, and happiness make their everyday lives tough and stressful because, unfortunately, we live in a society where money is very necessary. It is a medium to obtain the goods you need to facilitate life—simple things like a nice home to raise a family, quality food to put into your body, transportation, and an unpretentious, relaxing family vacation through which to experience different places on the beautiful earth we inhabit.

Money alone will not make you happy, but it is a vehicle to make your life a lot less complicated. Unfortunately, the uninstructed and financially illiterate poor and middle classes do not believe they can achieve financial freedom. Their money consciousness and money thermometer are very poor. Everyone has a money thermometer that gauges the level of wealth they consciously and subconsciously know and believe they can achieve. Some people have a money thermometer that is set at 40k per year, others at 400k per year, others at four million per year, and still others at 400 million per year. It is all based on your limiting beliefs and prevalent thoughts. We will discuss in a later chapter how to reprogram and move up your money thermometer to match your goals.

A huge problem with my parents, like that of the majority of poor and middle-class families, is that they love to tell their kids things like, "Money does not grow on trees," "You must work hard all your life in order to survive," "Rich people are crooks," "Money is the root of all evil." "You must go to college to get a good job," "Save your money and live below your means," "Invest in a 401k so that you have money for retirement." These are just a few of the many limiting beliefs that are programmed into 95% of society by their upbringing.

Our loved ones do not do this intentionally; they want the best for you, but it is very difficult to guide someone down a path of success and financial freedom if you have never been there yourself. It is like the uneducated financial advisors who give their clients financial advice that wipes out the clients' entire 401k and life savings; many of these financial advisors did not know what they were doing. The blind leading the blind is a recipe for disaster.

The conversations that rich and wealthy families have at the dinner table are a lot different from the conversations that poor and middle-class families have. The rich and wealthy are talking about buying and selling businesses, what the new hot investment trend is, investing in real estate, where they will be vacationing, what book they are reading, etc.

Completely different conversations go down at poor and middle-class dinner tables. The conversations are about finding a better job, overwhelming credit card debt, late rent, cars that need a new gadget, video games, the hottest gossip on TV, potential bill collectors calling, etc. There is a lot of tension about money-related matters in these conversations—tension that you carry into your adult life.

The sad thinking that has been passed down from generation to generation in low- and middle-class families is that you need to sacrifice the majority of your life "working hard" and then maybe, just maybe, you may be fortunate to live long enough to retire and to have saved enough to enjoy your life a little before you die.

I am here to assure you that this is not the "FasTrak" and that there is a more sound and successful thinking process. You have the ability, you have the opportunity to break the cycle, to break the chains that have mentally enslaved previous generations of your family.

The WealthPreneur Strategy will explain how you can reprogram this thinking one piece at a time and how I, as well as many low- and middle-class individuals, have been able to reprogram their thinking from limited to limitless. All you need to do is be willing and follow the process step by step, so be prepared to take action!

CHAPTER 2-EMPOWERING RE-CIRCUITING EXERCISES

Our brains are exponentially more powerful than a computer hard drive, but we as humans tap into only a very small portion of them. It is very easy to manipulate the brain, which is what the mainstream media does, whether we know it or not. Just like a computer, our brains can be hacked if we allow the wrong thoughts to enter and be programmed into our hard drives.

You can get lousy viruses in your brain and acquire a thinking process that will prevent you from achieving your goals and the levels of success you desire.

New research reveals the astonishing power of the brain to create, heal, and evolve. Scientists once believed that the brain's hardwiring couldn't be changed, but we now know that the brain is constantly evolving, and that our ability to reprogram our brains remains intact from birth to the end of life. With the right process and proven exercises, re-circuiting of the brain can be done repeatedly throughout the human life span. Researchers have also dispelled the myth that aging in the brain and memory loss are inevitable and irreversible. No matter how old we are, our brains are incredibly resilient and have the capacity to create new neural pathways if we choose to keep learning and opening ourselves to new experiences.

We have discovered more about the brain in the last five years than we had in the previous 500 years combined. Due to neuro-plasticity research, we now can actually see inside of the brain and analyze chemical imbalances as well as neuro circuit patterns. For the last seven years I have done extensive research on the mind, the human brain, and how they work. Scientific research and findings, along with my own experimenting, have given me cutting-edge insights into reprogramming the subconscious mind.

We had no choice about the programming that was passed down from our parents, whether good or bad. Now, as an independently thinking adult, you do have a choice, and you deserve to live a life by design, not by default.

Another big reason for this book is for the reader to understand that if you decide to change your programming and if you have the WILL and desire to create the life of your dreams, you can do it as long as you learn the coding language for rewiring your mind.

Just like there is coding language for cleaning out a virus in a computer hard drive, there are coding exercises for you to clean up the thoughts in your mind and ultimately take control of your life!

So let's start with the first lesson: your need to understand that THOUGHTS lead to ACTIONS, and actions lead to OUTCOMES. The outcomes or results determine the life you are currently living. The formula is T.A.O; first you have a T.hought; that thought leads you to commit an A.ction, and that action turns into an O.utcome. Outcomes shape the quality of life you live.

If you have limiting thoughts running in your subconscious all day long, a negative mindset and disbelief in what you are capable of accomplishing, your outcome is simply not going to be in your life's best interest.

For example, let's say that you have programmed into your subconscious the thought that you can make only 40k per year. That is a virus that is not going away, and that will keep you from ever making more than 40k per year, year after year until you reprogram a different belief system that empowers you and aligns with what you truly want. That is because all the thoughts you have will lead to actions that will have an outcome of 40k per year.

The crazy part of all this is that most people have no clue that the reason they don't earn more is because they have a virus in their subconscious mind that was passed down by their upbringing. This vicious thinking cycle is the reason top earners consistently earn high wages and low earners consistently earn low wages—because that's how their thermometers are set.

Most of us live in this cycle year after year, not realizing that it's because our thoughts need to be rewired! You are walking around with a virus, and the more time that passes, the more it spreads. Those of us who were not privileged enough to grow up in households that wired us to succeed need to seek books and experts like myself to teach us how to do it.

Okay, so since thoughts lead to actions and actions lead to outcomes, what you have to do is simply change your thoughts, which are at the root of everything. Once you change your thoughts, something very powerful happens; your actions get you better and more desirable results. The best part of all is that when you start achieving better outcomes, these outcomes start shaping and programming your subconscious.

The ultimate goal of rewiring your mind is to be able to have everything you want out of life programmed into your subconscious because your subconscious works a lot harder than your vision does. Once you correctly program your subconscious, the life of your dreams starts revealing itself AUTOMATICALLY.

The alignment of your subconscious with your goals will start creating the right circumstances and put in front of you the ideal people required to fulfill your dreams. When all of these events start unraveling, it is very important that you take the opportunities and know what to do with them. We will discuss this in later chapters— how to take advantage of the opportunities that come your way.

Now let's talk a little more on what you need to do to reprogram your thoughts. When creating a strong goal and rewiring the mind, you need to know that the "HOW" (how you will accomplish something) always reveals itself once you know the "WHAT." Therefore, when setting a powerful, life-changing goal, the most important thing you need to be clear on in your mind is the "'WHAT." What is it you specifically want to accomplish? In what time frame? The WHAT needs to be clear and descriptive.

Once you articulate WHAT, you want to write it down and then memorize it.

There are four key components of reordering and reprogramming your thinking and mind; these empower you to allow the human coding to happen. I call these key components R.A.V.E., which stands for:

1. **R**epetition
2. **A**ccomplishment
3. **V**isualization
4. **E**motion

These are very crucial in recoding your thoughts and imprinting your subconscious with new empowering beliefs that will shape your life to levels of success. You must do these exercises daily. Every single person I personally know who is wealthy and successful practices exercises similar to the ones I will demonstrate to you.

If all of them do it, if thousands of self-made millionaires can attest to something of this nature, do you think it works?

Just in case the virus in your brain is debating the answer, I will tell you that the answer is YES! It works. I am living proof. I come from a nice, loving family, but when it comes to money, health, wealth, and success, they programmed my young mind with every negative virus known to man. Through these daily exercises, I was able to break away from the limiting beliefs and re-circuit my thoughts and subconscious.

Attention! The exercises that allowed me to rewire my thoughts will empower you to take your life to the next level and are not to be taken lightly. I still practice these mechanisms daily. I want you all to mirror these exercises; the only difference will be that you will plug in your own goals and agendas. The blueprint has been created for you; all you have to do is personalize each coding exercise to fit your vision.

Do these every single morning in your car on your way to work or at home in a quiet room before you start your day. If you can, do them once in the morning and once at night, but in the beginning at least, practice these every morning before you start your day.

Exercise 1- Gratefulness

The feeling and emotion of gratitude is one of the most powerful (if not THE most powerful) human vibrations that will resonate in your mind, heart, and spirit, and that will help re-schedule your thoughts and subconscious. Think of every single thing you have to be thankful for, all the small things. The fact that you have eyes, ears, and the ability to be taking in the information in this book validates to me that you have a lot to be thankful for.

Another very key point in this exercise is to be thankful for everything you want in life. You have to be thankful for it as if you already have it. For example, if you want a new house, you would say something like, "I am thankful for the new house that I have." This part is so mind-boggling because, thinking back to a lot of the things I did not have that I used to be thankful for, I now have. Here is what I say every morning, verbatim:

"I am thankful for my life. I am thankful for my wife. I am thankful for my kids. I am thankful for my family. Everyone is healthy. Everyone is prosperous. I am thankful for my health. I am thankful for my excellent physique. I am thankful for my life. I am thankful for my wealth. I am thankful for surroundings. I am thankful for the people I come in contact with. Everyone is positive, I am thankful for my knowledge. I am thankful for my wisdom. I am thankful for all my assets, the cars, houses, gold, silver, and investments. They help me live a peaceful life. I am thankful for my trips. I love exploring new places in this beautiful earth. I am thankful for my businesses. My businesses are booming. My businesses are helping people. My businesses are making money. My businesses are changing lives. I am thankful for my apartments; my apartments are helping people. I am thankful for my buildings. I am thankful for my hotels. I am thankful for my vision. I am thankful for my Kids Foundation. My organization is financially educating poor kids around the world. I am thankful for the trucks, the trucks full of food. I get to feed the needy. I get to feed the hungry. I am giving them food, clothes, and shelter and financially educating them. I am thankful for my life. I am thankful for everything and everyone around me. I am absolutely blessed in every area of my life. I am thankful for the creator."

I have been reciting this specific exercise for the last three years every single morning; that is more than 1,000 consecutive days of repetition. Do you think it may be pretty well-programmed into my subconscious by now? I like doing this exercise in the car on my way to my office along with two other exercises that I will go over with you next.

It is amazing that the majority of the thoughts in that exercise I can proudly say I have accomplished. I constantly keep adding new ideas into this exercise and new manifestations of goals that I desire. I'm thankful for everything as if I have already obtained and achieved it. Do you think you would feel good each morning psychologically, physiologically, emotionally, energetically? Would you feel ready to take on and crush the rest of your day after that exercise? That is just the beginning!

So, quick analysis of this first exercise is that in order for it to imprint into your subconscious, you have to apply the **R.A.V.E** method. **R.epeat** it daily a few times per day. Work toward **A.ccomplishing** the manifestations you are being thankful for, which you have not yet obtained. Your thoughts will start changing, and therefore, so will your actions. The actions will be moving you toward achieving your goals. **V.isualize** yourself already accomplishing and owning the items you are thankful for as you are reciting them out loud. Last but definitely not least, you need to be passionate and have strong **E.motions** as you declare these exercises. Emotion ties everything together and neuro-links the thoughts of gratitude you are visualizing into your subconscious.

Neuro-linking is a strategy that will take your neuro-coding to a level of high performance. Take advantage of this powerful technique that was discovered with new, cutting-edge brain research and development. The process works as follows. You think of an event in your life when you were very happy, when you felt accomplished and successful. This could have been years ago, but you still vividly remember every detail of that event.

For example, the event could be winning a championship game in which you were the MVP. It could be a business accomplishment or any sort of success you had in life that made you feel outstanding.

Start visualizing that moment from the past that made you extremely happy and proud of yourself. Remember the emotions you felt that day, what you were wearing, the smells in the atmosphere. Keep that emotion as you start declaring a positive incantation, i.e., an affirmation like "I am healthy," "I am smart." What happens is that your brain starts neuro-linking that emotion from the past into your present statement. This technique is very powerful, and I can affirm to you that it works.

The coding it allows into your subconscious is absolutely magnificent because now your subconscious links the emotions, the vibrations, the chemical substances like protein and dopamine from that great memory to the affirmations of "I am brilliant" and "I am healthy and wealthy" that you are speaking out loud and simultaneously visualizing in your present. That is how you create real imprinting and start designing your life. You need to mentally create your life and then do the necessary work to materialize your thoughts. In later chapters, I will teach you how to materialize the vision that you are creating. We will go from A to Z, step by step.

So, let's get into exercise number two, during which we will be implementing the neuro-linking strategy.

Exercise 2- "Genius Empowerments"

I always follow this exercise after being thankful for all that I have and all that I will have. In this exercise you will be asserting a lot of encouraging qualities about yourself that you currently possess or that you want to possess, but remember: We declare everything as if we already possess it. We own it.

I will go over what I do and what I say for this exercise; you can fine-tune it to meet your goals and aspirations. Before I start saying this exercise, I take a trip down memory lane to a moment when I felt very proud of myself early in my career. It was the first week of the year, and I had finished the previous year as the number-one sales agent in the company out of hundreds of agents. I was only twenty years of age. A new year had started and everyone was motivated to beat me that year. They wanted to take down my number-one spot since I had outperformed everyone else by quite a huge gap. To give you an idea, I made about six figures more than the person who was number two for that year. So having this target on my back, I challenged myself to a huge goal that to everyone else seemed unrealistic. They couldn't even fathom the goal I was going for. I wanted to engage more than twenty new clients to the law firm in one week—five business days. I wanted to do this the first week of the year.

The deadline for all client submissions was Thursday night, and everyone got to see the huge, long sales ranking report every Friday morning. I remember walking in Friday morning with a brand-new suit and going up the elevator to the top floor of the building, which was the sales floor.

Knowing what I had accomplished, I walked in. Everyone who had seen the ranking report, which ranked every agent from one to 150, looked at me and smiled. Executives and colleagues alike were celebrating me and showing me well-earned respect. The ranking report showed Ruddy Palacios at number one with twenty-two engagements in one week. That was equivalent to a good month for the average agent. I felt happy, proud, and successful. I had made over 8,300 USD plus a few bonuses in a week and had broken all company records. I sent a clear message to everyone that I planned to stay consistent. Not bad for a twenty-year-old Hispanic kid with no formal education. That month I made about 30K and was consistent the whole year.

So when I proclaim the words in this exercise, I am thinking of that day and neuro-linking those emotions and feelings into my new ideas and thoughts. These are the exact words I recite each morning:

"I am a brilliant, savvy, and genius businessman, I have all the resources, all the contacts, and all the money in the world. I am a happy, healthy, wealthy multi-millionaire. I have an abundant mindset. I am an excellent money manager. I am vividly creative and an innovator. I am an excellent mentor and coach to others. I am a wise parent, loving father and husband. I have magnificent problem-solving skills. I am a sharp investor and great communicator. I am a clever negotiator. Everything I need and want comes to me easily. I am loved by everyone I connect with. I was created for greatness. I live a fulfilled life with purpose and significance."

This exercise is good to practice every morning as you are getting ready for the day, preferably in the mirror so that you can see yourself as you declare these incantations. This is very powerful when done correctly and will start shifting your mindset and recoding your brain's hard drive. Daily repetition will allow this to submerge itself into your subconscious. When you do anything enough times, it becomes automatic. The goal is for all these affirmations to become automatic and second nature to who you are as a person.

I want to give you a "simple stupid" illustration of how powerful the subconscious part of our minds is once it's programmed. Have you ever gotten into your car and, without thinking about it, safely driven yourself home? You didn't need a map or GPS. You didn't need to work hard thinking about what you needed to do to get home or how you were going to maneuver the vehicle. You could have been listening to music, talking to a friend in the car, thinking about a million other things, and somehow you still got home. You probably have even thought about it. Why? Because it's automatic! It is second nature to you because you have driven home so many times; you simply get in your car after work and you don't think; your subconscious just drives you home.

Imagine that you can achieve the life of your dreams as easily as it is for a normal, sober adult to drive themselves home. No matter how many cars (obstacles) are on the road to your house, you can typically make it home fairly easy. Your subconscious maneuvers through traffic, lights, signs, etc. basically on autopilot. When you implement these techniques repeatedly until they become automatic, the road to the life of your dreams will not only be easy, it will be the FasTrak!

Thoughts become actions and actions become outcomes, which are what blossom into the life you are currently living. If you want a better life, you need to cultivate and plant better thoughts. You need to repeatedly take control of your conscious thoughts so that your subconscious thoughts are working toward creating the life you desire and deserve. This is why immediate implementation of these exercises is crucial to re-circuit your mind.

Exercise 3- "Giving Vibrations"

The next exercise is one that promotes the vibration for giving. In life there is a beautiful equation known as cause and effect. When you input giving and receiving into that formula of cause and effect, it becomes very easy to understand that if you give (i.e., the cause), the receiving will be the effect. This works wonderfully, and it feels magnificent to give. Even if you give without expecting anything in return, it always comes back to you many times multiplied.

It is like a law, and the ultra-rich understand this. That is why Bill Gates and his foundation give away more money than any other billionaire alive. Warren Buffet gives his money to the Bill Gates Foundation because he like the causes it donates to. The more these two give, the more they receive. Bill Gates literally makes more money in his sleep than most millionaires do all year working.

The emotion you capture from giving to a cause you believe in is very powerful. It positively shapes your programming to that of abundance. It gives you an insight that there is enough to go around. Giving is a huge problem for people who have limiting beliefs because they want to hoard everything for themselves; they have a mindset of scarcity.

When I say give, I don't just mean money; this can be food, shelter, information, love, books, your time, etc. The act of giving is making a difference in someone's life.

Let's jump into Exercise 3, once again focusing on repeating it a few times daily. This is what I say every morning verbatim:

"I now command my subconscious mind to direct me into helping as many people as humanly possible. In giving me the strength, the power, the love, the understanding, the humor, the brevity, the passion, the compassion, the patience, and whatever else it takes to show these people and get these people to change their lives right now. I want to impact every life that I come across in a positive way. I want to help people. I want to change people's lives for the better and the best!"

I repeat this incantation over and over again every morning with passion and great emotion. I believe this exercise has subconsciously led me to write this book. Cool realizations as I write this!

These three exercises alone will shift and completely rewire your thoughts and current limiting beliefs.

CHAPTER 3-THE POWER OF POSITIVE PROGRAMMING

Positive programming is a world of difference from positive thinking. Positive programming is effective, strategic, scientific, tested, and life-changing. It empowered my life. Positive thinking is just simple thinking; you can think all day long and get zero results.

The positive coding techniques I will reveal in this chapter are highly effective. They enabled my students as well as myself to accomplish amazing achievements.

I want you to begin to strategically arrange pictures around your house, your car, and your place of work that promote abundance and the lifestyle you desire. Visualization is exceptionally influential on your subconscious. Visualization is a global language, and images and pictures are the universal dialect that your subconscious understands more quickly than verbal words.

For example, if you were in a country where no one spoke your language and you were looking for directions to the local bank, it would be very difficult for someone to understand what you were saying and looking for. However, if you showed that person a picture of the local bank with a question mark, your chances of them knowing what you were asking for are significantly higher. That is because images are a universal language.

The subconscious works similarly; it understands and processes pictures. The types of images you surround yourself with most often are the kind your neuro hard drive will attract more of because it is what you are inputting.

Just as if you go into a search engine like Bing or Yahoo for images and type in the word MONEY, instantly the search engine retrieves every single piece of information on that word –millions of results pop up for what you put into the search bar.

Knowing that neuro research says that the mind is like a search engine on steroids because it's much more complex and powerful, I have created a list of depictions and strategic placements of images to input into your daily life. Your subconscious should search for these, furthering the coding and programming. These strategies have been proven to work by many of my students, myself, and my mentors.

Here is a list of opportunities for visual programming that you can implement in your daily life. I still personally practice these today.

1. Strategically place money, coins, silver, hard assets, and checks around the house in places you visit often, like the kitchen, cabinets, closets, drawers you open daily, car, pockets, etc. You want to create a feeling of abundance and not scarcity.

2. Create a "Vision Board" of all the material and spiritual experiences you want to acquire during your lifetime. You want to strategically place this in locations where you will see it daily.

3. Take ten minutes daily to sit down and meditate. Take deep breaths and visualize the perfect day from the time you wake up to the time you go to sleep. Where would you be and with whom? What activities would you partake in? How would you feel? Be as descriptive as possible.

4. Each day, take out a clean sheet of paper and write down your income goal for retirement and in how many years you want to retire. Take fifteen minutes out of your day to think of four new, innovative ideas that can potentially help you toward your goal. That's twenty-eight new ideas per week. Have an idea file; all it takes is one great idea well-executed to make you wealthy. I will elaborate on this more in later chapters.

5. Set daily reminders into your cell phone for all the above exercises. This is one of the many advantages we have with technology; as soon as you see the reminder, do not think about it. Do not procrastinate. Just take action immediately; you already scheduled that time into your day for this activity.

No matter how smart you are, you will not remember to take action on all these exercises unless you are constantly reminded, and what better way to remind yourself than with an object that all of modern-day society is glued to like zombies? Most people will drive thirty minutes back home just to pick up their phones if they forget them, so I believe this is an effective way to keep up with your schedule and to take action on all the goals on your plate!

CHAPTER 4-THE WEALTH MINDSET

ATTENTION! Now that we have started to rewire the bad programming and viruses into positive, limitless hardware, it is time to start focusing on the next phase of the FasTrak to wealth, which is GOALS! Goals are the blueprints. They are what cause your brain to start looking for ways to get what you want. The masterminding goes on autopilot once it has a guide to where it wants to go and the direction desired.

Without goals there is no sense of direction regarding where and why you are traveling. When writing down your goals, you want to record WHAT you want, WHY you want it, and HOW you plan on achieving it. Once you feel strong about the "what" and the "why," the "how" always reveals itself. Why do you think this is important?

The reason is that when you descriptively write down the **what** and the **why**, they imprint into the coding of your conscious and subconscious brain. Goals are simply plans of action that you must follow like a map.

Do you know of any superstructures or state-of-the-art architecture that was built without a well-thought-out blueprint? It takes engineers months of planning and writing out ideas and designs before they even get started, and this is all done for a building. Do you think your life deserves the same attention to detail? Is your life important enough for this type of diligent planning? Is writing out how you are going to execute and create the rest of your life mission critical? If your answer is YES, then you should have no problem sitting down and writing out all of your goals. I will go over some exercises and examples of how I write out my goals and how many of the most successful people on the planet do it as well.

To create the level of success and wealth you want to achieve, you need to focus and have a high grade of commitment. You need to sit down and figure out what it is that you want out of life and envision what the perfect life would be like. You must have specific health goals, career goals, love/relationship goals, family goals, contribution-to-society goals, intellectual growth goals, spiritual development goals, and business and financial goals. In this book we will focus on the financial and wealth-building aspects of your goals. We will start with the specific income goal that will allow you to retire. What is the amount of money you need to generate residually, meaning whether you work or not, in order to obtain financial freedom?

Once you have that number in mind, you need to write it down and begin to focus on it daily. Come up with ideas that will move you toward that goal. The best way to concentrate and accomplish a goal is to track it, as what you focus on and track will expand.

The best way to track your goals is the same way large companies track their goals, which is by breaking them down, typically into quarters. Let's assume that you are a beginner and have never written down any goals.

The first thing you need to do is come up with your current net worth. Your net worth is the value of all your assets, minus the total of all your liabilities. An easy way to calculate your net worth is what is owned minus what is owed. Your net worth is what you would have in cash if you sold every significant possession and paid off all your debts.

Calculate that number no matter what it currently is; it may even be negative if you have a lot of debt. Where you start or where you currently are financially is irrelevant because through the mechanisms taught in this book, if you implement them, we will get you to that number. That desired goal you want to accomplish will be very attainable in your near future.

Grab a piece of paper and let's start writing some goals.

What is your goal for your net worth in the next twelve months? (Remember, what you focus on expands.)

How much active income (active income is money you make from working a job or your own business, trading time for money) do you want to make in the next twelve months?

How much residual income (i.e., passive income) do you want to earn in the next twelve months? (You generate passive income from investments, interest on money from active income, real estate, businesses, etc. If you are a beginner and have no clue about these things, don't worry about it. I have you covered. That is what we will discuss toward the end of this book.)

Once you have a number for each of those questions and you have solidified as well as written down each of your goals, you need to chunk it down. Break down each goal into quarters; like all large corporations, you are breaking down the goal into four parts.

The first quarter is what you plan to accomplish in the first three months, e.g., January to March.

The second quarter is the following three months, April to June.

The third quarter is July to September, and last but not least,

the fourth quarter is October to December.

Your months can be different depending on when you decide to start, but the idea is to break down your yearly goal into quarters to track your progress.

When creating your goals, you need to think short-term and long-term. You need to have a vision for the future and a strong plan for instant action. You need to ask yourself powerful and meaningful questions. Take your time answering these questions.

Here is a list of mission-critical, important questions; I want you to sit and write these questions down. Write down as much as you can for each answer; be as descriptive as possible. This could be the most meaningful exercise of your entire life. This is the one thing that could make ALL the difference in your life. As you answer these questions and visualize the answers, you will be imprinting your conscious and subconscious mind. You will literally be designing your life one question after the next.

Here is a huge wealth nugget: Why is it that only about 5% of all human beings are actually financially free and live the lives of their dreams? The answer is that the majority of people never take the time to sit down and take an exercise like this very seriously.

They are okay with working forty hours per week in a low-paying job building someone else's dream, but to take forty hours to sit down and design their own dream is not worth their time. Doesn't that sound absolutely ridiculous?

Yet the majority of society lives this way and goes on just getting by. DO NOT MAKE THIS MISTAKE! TAKE THIS SERIOUSLY. You owe it to yourself, to your family, and your future generations of loved ones. Even if it took you hours, days, weeks, months to fully answer every question with passion and emotion, is it worth it? Can you do it? Will it work? The answer is YES!

Okay, so here we go. Strap into your seat, put on your thinking cap, be creative, and most importantly, think big when designing your life. You should be extremely excited to know that these goals/thoughts/ideas will materialize once you know what they are and once you focus on achieving them each and every day.

A. My perfect life:

- What is a perfect day in my perfect life if money and time were not an object?
- What is the first thing I'll do when I get out of bed?
- What will I listen to? Read? Research? Explore?
- What exercises will I do?
- What will I eat?
- How will I relax? What will that feel like?
- What is my health and physique like?
- How do I reward myself? What music will be playing?
- What do I create?

- What am I thankful for?

- What is my mental and physical state?

- Who will be there with me?

- What are they adding to my life? How, specifically?

- Where will I be? Country, town, environment?

- What does my home look like inside and out?

- What smells and aromas are in the air?

- What are my plans for the morning, afternoon, and evening?

- Who are my mentors and in what are they mentoring me?

- What mentors who have helped me in the past am I still thankful for?

- What am I able to do better than anyone else? What are my strengths/talents?

- What am I an expert at?

- What knowledge do I have that others seek?

- What will I get out of living my perfect day?

- How will I feel? What will I have accomplished?

You will find out so much about yourself as you are going through these questions. Take your time and really think about each answer. Close your eyes and go to a relaxing setting as you answer these questions—the beach would be a good place, or even somewhere with a nice view. Let's continue designing your new life.

B. My perfect career or business (Imagination is key. "Imagine"– Einstein):

- What perfect career/business have I created/built for myself?

- Why did I create/build this career/business?

- What do I get from my career or business? Money? Satisfaction? Recognition?
- How much money? How much satisfaction? How much recognition?
- Is it enough?
- What am I giving back to my family? City? State? Country? Humanity? Universe?
- How do I feel when I experience my career daily? Excited? Fulfilled?
- How did I get to this place in my life?
- What did I learn?
- What did I experience?
- What did I create?
- How did what I learn, experience, and create tie together to get to this perfect situation?
- How big is my career? Am I in control?
- When will my career or business be complete?
- How will I know specifically when I've achieved all that I should?
- How did I create my perfect career or business? What did I do specifically?
- Who helped me?
- How did I meet those people?
- What did they get out of helping me?
- What am I known for?
- What do my family and loved ones get from my career or business?

- What limitations, obstacles, or roadblocks did I overcome to get here?
- How did I overcome?
- How does my career or business fit into and support my perfect life?

The coding and wealth mindset that you will receive from these exercises is going to be astronomical in your evolution from an entrepreneur into a WealthPreneur. You are, in essence, on simulation mode for your soon-to-be new and improved life. Why do you think the military always has simulation combat? It has tons and tons of simulated tactic trainings that mirror real-life scenarios. The same thing goes for astronauts; they spend most of their lives training on simulators for maybe one or two space trips. The simulation and repetitive training allows them to execute the real-life scenario a lot easier and with few to no mistakes.

You are doing the same thing with these exercises; the only difference is that you are simulating your LIFE. You need to know and be confident that it is just a matter of time until you actually materialize everything you are writing down, envisioning, and imprinting into your subconscious mind. You will develop a sense of expectancy that it is just a matter of time until you experience these goals in the physical world which you have already experienced and been at in the metaphysical state of being.

Let's continue programming the wealth mindset.

My perfect relationship:

- Who is the person in my life who completes me as a person?

- What qualities about that person make them perfect for me?
- What do they look like specifically?
- What do they love most about me?
- How are they brilliant?
- How do they complete me specifically? What do they add to the equation that I don't already have?
- What kind of person are they?
- What do they do for a living?
- How educated are they? Formally? Informally?
- What do they do for fun?
- What do they do for me that no one else on the planet can?
- How does my body feel when I am with them? How do my emotions feel?
- What do they know about me that no one else does?
- How do I show them how I love them? How do they react to that?
- What is our married life like?
- What friends will we have?
- How are our kids?
- What is our friendship like?
- What is our sex life like?
- What is our time apart like?
- What are our vacations like?
- Where do we go?
- What are we known for?
- What kind of music and movies do we watch together?
- What is the one dream they have that I support every way I can?

- What limiting beliefs, emotions, thoughts, or ideas did I overcome to attract the perfect partner?
- How did I overcome?
- How does my partner fit into my perfect life?

These questions are very critical in programming the wealth mindset because true wealth is having a balanced life that is fulfilled in every important human need. The next part is what most entrepreneurs like yourself are probably most interested in: designing the financial aspect of your life. However, it is important to be aware of and acknowledge that all areas of your life need to be designed and given attention.

Let's dive into designing your financial wealth.

My perfect financial situation:

- How much money do I have?
- How much wealth do I have? (investments, savings, etc.)
- What trappings of wealth do I have? (cars, homes, boats, yachts, planes, etc.)
- What does my wealth get me?
- How does my wealth make me feel?
- How do I use my wealth to make the world a better place?
- What is the next big thing I'll do with my money?
- How do I get my wealth?
- How do those around me feel about my wealth?
- What is something surprising I am able to do with money?
- What things do I buy easily?
- How did my life change as a result of my wealth?
- What is my attitude about money? Why?

- If I need more money tomorrow, how do I get it?

- What does my money get for me?

- How specifically did I learn to have the wealth that I have? ANSWER WITH AS MANY WAYS AS YOU CAN.

- What do I study? What do I read? How often?

- Are there people in my life who help me with my money? What do those people do?

- How did I decide to have these people help me?

- What obstacles or limiting behaviors about money have I overcome?

- How did I overcome them?

- Am I leaving a legacy for my family?

- How will I be remembered and talked about?

- How does my wealth fit into My Perfect Life?

Here are the last few questions for programming your wealth mindset. Remember to stay focused, breathe, imagine, visualize, be creative, and believe that it is only a matter of time until what you are writing down materializes. I know that it has for me and for many others who have achieved a great deal of success in their lives.

- What is my life like twelve months from today? Financially and emotionally?

- What is my life like three years from today? Financially and emotionally?

- What is my life like seven years from today? Financially and emotionally?

- What is my life like ten years from today? Financially and emotionally?

These are the real mechanics behind truly mapping out your goals and having a blueprint of your future, something to really work toward. Once you have written out everything, you need to put this in a place where you can see your answers daily so that they serve as reminders of what you are working toward. Also remember that repetition programs your mind, so the more you review this, the quicker the programming will take place. These questions will get your frontal lobe working all day long. What I am going over with you is not a theory; the majority of this has now been proven by science and lab research.

I advise you to glance at your new goals and visions as often as possible. I suggest that you definitely sit down and go through everything you wrote down at least every few months; revise your goals, check off what you have achieved, and set new goals accordingly. You want to keep them current and alive in your mind.

What the mind can perceive it truly can achieve. If you don't believe me, just look around at all the technology, gadgets, cars, buildings, spaceships, etc. They were, once upon a time, just thoughts in someone's brain—thoughts that materialized in the physical world through hard work, focus, and STRATEGY.

That is what this book will enlighten you with. I am very excited for your near future and the amazing things you are going to accomplish due to your new programming. Now, if you get stuck for more than ten minutes on any one question, move on to the next one. You can come back to the questions you were not sure how to answer once you finish reading the entire book. I believe that after you finish reading this book, you will have much more clarity on every aspect of your life.

CHAPTER 5-THE SUPREME BRAIN

Now that you have encrypted the wealth mindset into your brain and mind, you will be walking around with a super brain. This is something that the majority of people around you do not have. They have virus-infected brains full of negative programming and limiting beliefs. You need to guard your brain and your new programming from being infected by the majority of negativity around you.

You will do this by forming new alliances with like-minded individuals. There are so many free groups you can join on meetup.com and many other platforms, like private clubs where you can find like-minded individuals.

Your brain contains about 100 billion nerve cells forming anywhere from a trillion to even a quadrillion connections, called synapses. These connections are in a constant, dynamic state of remodeling in response to the world around you. This may sound astonishing, but it is one of the least remarkable things the brain is responsible for.

Your brain not only interprets the world, it creates it. Everything you hear, see, taste, touch, and smell would have none of those qualities without the brain. The brain is the tool that God designed and created to be responsible in the physical world to materialize these things. Whatever you experience today—your morning WealthPreneur coffee, the love you feel for your family, a brilliant idea for your business—has been specifically customized solely for you.

Now, if your world is unique and customized for you and you alone, who is behind such remarkable creativity: you or the brain itself? If the answer is you, then the door to greater creativity is wide open.

We have entered a golden age of brain research. We have new breakthroughs coming up every month. Even the most sophisticated brain scans available would show no detectable difference between a Mozart and a brand-new musician. But the physical brain is not nearly the whole story.

To create a golden age for your brain, you need to use the gift that God the creator has given you in a new way. It's not the number of neurons or magic chemicals that makes life more inspiring and successful. Genes play their part, but your genes, like the rest of the brain, are also changing and evolving.

Every day you step into the invisible firestorm of electrical and chemical activity that is the brain's environment. You act as leader, innovator, entrepreneur, and user of your brain all at once.

As leader, you direct the daily orders to your brain.

As innovator, you create new pathways and connections inside your brain that didn't exist before.

As entrepreneur, you train your brain to learn and create new expertise.

As user, you are responsible for keeping your brain functioning properly.

When you have a Super Brain and are using it correctly, you are a fully aware creator using the brain to its maximum advantage. Your brain can adapt limitless times; when you put it to work, you will achieve far more fulfilling results than you are currently achieving. If you implement everything in this book, you will truly put your brain to work and achieve the potential for which it was created.

Having a Super Brain is a privilege, so do not take it lightly. You need to use it for the greater good and affect as many lives as possible in a positive way. You need to start living a life of significance, transferring your gifts to others and empowering infected, negative-programmed brains to change their programming and live the lives of their dreams.

A vital component of keeping your Super Brain healthy and programmed with abundance is meditation. There are hundreds of books on meditation. There are many local venues that have meditation groups that will teach you how to meditate. The meditation I like to practice is transcendental meditation, which is known as one of the most powerful forms of meditation, but any meditation in which you sit down and focus on your breathing and nothing else for any considerable period of time will empower and enrich your brain.

You want to start off with just five minutes. Even if you think you can do more, take baby steps. Once you have consistently meditated for five minutes after seven days, you can incrementally start doing it for longer periods of time. Train your brain little by little; trust me, this is one of the most powerful exercises you can do in your lifetime. It allows you to disconnect from the physical world and enables you to connect with the energy of the universe. I called it God, but you can call it whatever you want.

One thing I do know is that most of the greatest men and women who have walked this earth, legends of our ancestry, have all done some sort of meditation technique that disconnected them from the physical being and connected them with true energy and a higher power greater than they were. Through this book I want to spark that thought in your brain. Do your own research on it, but seriously look into it. I am not a meditation expert, so I won't get into it any further. I am a mindset and business strategy expert, but trust me; to live a balanced life, it is all relevant, and you need to be exposed to it.

Congratulations! You have experienced the first move in the WealthPreneur Strategy; programming your mind is a crucial step toward becoming a WealthPreneur. There is a very important reason why it is step number one; if you do not get this step right, the rest of the steps will not work to their full potential. You need to think like a millionaire, feel like a millionaire, and see like a millionaire before you actually become one. Wealth must be created in your mind first.

If you physically get a million dollars before building your wealth mindset and a strong foundation, you will more likely than not be back to broke in a very short period of time. The majority of lottery winners go broke about twenty-four months after winning millions of dollars. The same thing happens with the majority of athletes and many celebrities. So take this step very seriously because the following steps in the following chapters will allow you to make a tremendous amount of money. However, if you don't build your foundation mentally, you will not be able to manage and keep that money. So let's make it, keep it, and create wealth.

Now that we have the correct mindset, confidence, and moral character, and you understand the mechanics of the inner game of wealth, you possess all these great qualities. Let's move into the next power moves that you need to make to become a WealthPreneur in the physical world. These mechanical and physical moves will allow you to turn your positive programming and thoughts into reality. The next move is POSITIONING your business and raising capital; this is how we get money and funding for our businesses, products, ideas, dreams, etc.

PART 2

Positioning Your Business for Funding & Raising Capital

CHAPTER 6-INCORPORATING YOUR BUSINESS THE RIGHT WAY!

Warning! This next power move is absolutely critical in order for you to go from an average entrepreneur into a WealthPreneur. People I meet everywhere, via social media, meetings, conferences, or just day-to-day life, always ask me, "I have a few thousand dollars. What should I do. What should I invest it in?" A lot of gurus would say to start investing in XY and Z. They sell a dream that your $3000 will turn into millions if you invest in them or with them.

I tell my students, start a business. What I mean by starting a business is incorporate yourself, become a legal entity. The average American does not even know what a legal entity is, let alone know how they can be extremely advantageous to have and control. So what is a legal entity?

The politically correct definition for it is "An association, corporation, partnership, proprietorship, trust, or individual that has legal standing in the eyes of law." A legal entity has legal capacity to enter into agreements or contracts, assume obligations, incur and pay debts, sue and be sued in its own right, and to be held responsible for its actions.

My definition of it is that when you incorporate a business, you the individual give birth to a real being; existent with no expiration date, corporations can live forever and be passed on from generation to generation. It is an organization or being that possesses separate existence for tax purposes. When you incorporate, your business will have its own Social Security number, called an Employer Identification Number (EIN); having that is very powerful if you use it wisely.

I am going to teach you the easiest way to incorporate a business and take you step by step through how you will be able to present, package, and position your business to obtain business lines of credits, credit cards with high available credit at 0% interest, money from private investors/private parties, and ultimately all the funding you will need to create the business of your dreams.

The way you structure your corporation is essential in raising capital. The way I am going to coach you to build your corporation will allow banks, lending institutions, and private investors to take your business seriously. You as a small business need to present yourself like a Walmart, a Starbucks, and all these other big corporations.

This is why I advise my students to get incorporated first, because there are so many advantages of incorporating and building your business credit report profile so that you are fundable and verifiable. Not only will you have access to hundreds of thousands of dollars, if you structure everything correctly, you will be protected in many ways from legal liability. You will be able to have huge tax savings and live the corporate lifestyle, which is a whole lot more advantageous than living as a normal, hard-working individual. Corporations have so many laws swinging in their favor. Huge corporations spend millions of dollars lobbying to get these laws passed in their favor so you can piggyback off of them and learn to play the game. I will not get into specifics on how you can be protected from legal liability or how incorporating will help you with tax savings. Seek a lawyer and a CPA for the details on how you can benefit.

If you become one of my coaching students in the WealthPreneur Club, I refer you to good attorneys and CPAs who can counsel you and give you a free consultation.

I am not giving you legal advice or tax advice. I just want to make you aware and state simple facts that when you become an entity, there is liability protection in many different ways, and potential tax savings. If you research what Google and Starbucks pay for taxes, it will be an eye-opener.

So this is why I say if you only have a few thousand dollars, no matter what investment vehicle you put it into, it will not make you rich or wealthy. To start creating wealth, you need to have a few hundred thousand, preferably a million plus USD to invest in a residual income vehicle that will yield a reasonable return. Enough passive income to sustain your lifestyle.

What I am saying is if you have $10,000 you cannot live very well off of $10,000 USD paying you 10% net annualized interest because that means you will only get about $83 per month. Take that same return on investment and apply it to $500,000 USD or $1,000,000 USD getting 10% net annualized interest, the $500,000 will pay you about $4,100 per month. The $1,000,000 will pay you about $8,300 per month.

That is residual income that can support most people's lifestyle without working again -- decent amount of money in your sleep. If you want to live a more luxurious lifestyle, then you simply need to make more money, get to several million, and invest it into passive income strategies.

This is the way to get on the FasTrak instead of what most Americans are doing, which is trying to save several thousand per year, collect a little interest for forty years, and hopefully retire with enough to live on in their sixties. That is modern-day slavery in my eyes. The WealthPreneur strategy will get you on a FasTrak pathway to freedom.

So how do you get to the few hundred thousand or the few million to invest into passive income vehicles? Depending on how ambitious you are, you may only need get to a few hundred thousand or, if you are very ambitious, a few million. I will coach you through the action steps you need to take in the remainder of this book.

The first action step you need to take is incorporating your business the right way. This will allow you to get access and tap into as much money as you need. There is a system to structure your business so that it becomes fundable, meaning when a bank, a lending institution, or private investor looks at your business, it is packaged correctly, professional, presentable, all the paperwork is in order, and most importantly, your business has a high business credit score. This shows anyone you are seeking money from that your business has the ability to pay. Therefore they will typically trust you with any amount of money that you request.

Let's talk about incorporating the right way! What we are building is a funding corporation, "which is a corporation that will be designed specifically to obtain financing and money to fund your ideas, projects, and potential high-yield investments."

So when setting up this type of entity, the name that you pick is very important. You want to pick a short, easy name that has absolutely no meaning, almost a made-up word if you will.

For example, Google, Nokia, Netflix, IKEA, and Amazon, etc. These are very easy, generic names that do not mean anything. You want to come up with something similar; the reason why is because you do not want your name to give away what it is that your business does.

You do not want names like Smith Real Estate Group Inc., Harold's Auto Body Corp. These names tell the banks and lending institutions what kind of industry you are in. If it is a risky industry they are already very unlikely to lend to you. Another very important reason for a simple, generic name is that if your business wants to change what they do, or they go into different industries, a generic name works for any.

You want to be the one who tells people what exactly your business does, not them assume by your name, so the name should give them no clue what it is you do. Now when telling them what you do, you want to pick an industry that is considered "safe" to lending institutions. Every single industry has a rating based on all the business credit reports gathered by Dun & Bradstreet which is an international business credit reporting agency. They rank business based on what industry pays their bills late or on time, what industry is most likely to file BK, the types of business that default thirty days, sixty days, ninety days, etc. We will talk a little more about D&B in a later chapter. For now let's stick to the task at hand, picking a safe industry.

The safest industry that has the best rating is "business management services" or "marketing and advertising". Every industry is classified by a specific code. There are two types of codes used for tracking types of business industries. One type of business industry tracking code is called Standard Industrial Classification, "SIC". The other one is called the North American Industry Classification System, "NAICS". This is the one that is most used in this day and age.

So you want to incorporate your business under business management services, which is SIC code: 8741 and NAICS code: 541611. Any industry that you are in can do business management of some sort. Some of my students are interior designers, so they manage their business and also help others manage their interior design business; other students do IT work so their business is going to manage others' IT departments. My first business was doing sales trainings for other businesses, so that is what I managed. So what kind of business do you want to help manage? The options are unlimited. I help my clients and students in my WealthPreneur Club pick all these things and advise them on what is best for their specific scenario, but you can do it yourself.

The names that you decide on you need to Google to see if another business has already taken that name, and then you need to look in your secretary of state website to see if that name is available. You definitely want your name to be unique; you don't want anyone else to have it.

Up to this point, you should have a name picked out and know what industry your business will be classified under. We are doing all these preliminary steps before going and actually filing the corporation with the state, which I'll go over with you as well. I have a very easy way to do it. The next thing you need to decide on is what is going to be your business address. Depending on your starting financial situation you have a few options.

Option #1 you can use your home address as your corporate address. Option #2 you can rent out a virtual office through Regus.com which will run you anywhere from $70-$120 per month depending on the location. Option #3 you can rent out an actual office space which will range in price depending on size and location.

So depending on your finances, any one of those will work for our "funding corporation" purposes.

Once you establish the name, industry, and address, you need to obtain a corporate phone number. There are many different options for this. The one I have found the easiest and most inexpensive is Vonage. You want to pick a local area code, not a 1(800) number because one paramount step of this process is to get your business listed on 411, Yellow Pages, and all the 411 directories. A local area code will facilitate that. You want your business to be visible. Vonage will charge you about $40 USD per month.

Once you have those initial items for your business, which are a well-researched corporate name, industry, corporate address (headquarters), and corporate phone number, you are ready to incorporate with your local state. The best and easiest way to do this is by calling a company that specializes in correctly filing the paperwork for you and incorporating your business with the state.

I send all my friends and students to a company called "Mycorporation.com". The CEO is a good friend of mine. They are very good at what they do. It is very inexpensive for them to do all the paperwork and filing for you. This is the stress-free, easy route to incorporating. Depending on what state you are in, the fees are anywhere from $100-$400. Most attorneys charge over $3,000 just to file your corporation, and they typically have their paralegals do it, who fill in the blank forms.

Save your money and go this route. Mention my name to Mycorporation.com and they may even give you a discount. The CEO, Deborah Sweeney, is an awesome person. You can do it online with them, but I think if you are a beginner, it is best to call them, and one of their representatives will walk you through everything over the phone.

For the purposes of building a "funding corporation", I typically tell my students to go with a C-corporation. You can tell them that when they ask what kind of entity you want to form, they will make the process smooth and easy. You also want to buy something called a "corporate kit", which will have all your required corporate filings and all internal documents for your business.

Once you file and incorporate your business with the state, it takes about two weeks for you to hear back from them that the business has been officially filed. At this point you will receive a package in the mail along with your corporate kit and something called the "articles of incorporation". You want to make sure you have a designated area that is secure but also easy for you to access, for all of your corporate documents.

In the meantime, while you are waiting for them to get back to you, there is a lot of work you need to get moving on. The next step is to buy the domain for your business name. I recommend buying your domain with Godaddy.com. You can buy your business name domain for about $1 per month or $12 per year. You want to set up a very simple but professional site using a free generic business management template that GoDaddy offers.

All you need to have on your website is your business name, address, the kind of services you provide, and how you can be contacted. Again, visibility is very important when building your "funding corporation". Also remember, how your business is perceived is very important. All banks and lending institutions will visit your site. They want to make sure you are a real business.

Another thing you want to buy with your site is website email. You need to have a professional email you provide banks, lending institutions, and investors. You do not want to give out your email when it is somethingsilly@gmail.com or @yahoo.com, etc. You are perceived as a legitimate and professional business when you give them an email like Jenifer@wealthpreneurgroup.com or Info@wealthpreneurgroup.com . You want to have at least two company emails to start, one that has your firstname@yourcompanyname.com and another that is info@yourcompanyname.com .

The point I want you to really grasp is that you need to start acting like a large, reputable business. Once you incorporate, you go from an average individual to a corporate lifestyle that you are in control of. You are the one in charge of designing your path.

Make sure you are putting out that image of a strong, professional, well-established business that knows exactly what they are doing. You need that powerful energy and confidence with everyone you come in contact with, the way you dress, the way you talk, the courtesy and respect you show to everyone.

Make sure you study all the concepts in this book and continue to educate yourself on business principles and commerce through other books, audio books, seminars, business coaching, and anything you can get your hands on that has a proven track record. I have a lot of resources on my website, www.thewealthstrategy.com, of recommended books and help to make sure you are business-competent when you are out there building this.

Okay, so now that you have your corporate website and your business emails set up, it is time to officially give birth to your entity/business. What officially gives your corporation life and existence is two things. Number one is the tax ID number, better known as "EIN", that is basically your business's Social Security number. Number two is opening up a corporate bank account.

It is very easy to complete both of these steps. To obtain your EIN, you can go online to www.IRS.gov and click on request EIN and just fill in the requested information on the form that populates. If you find that too confusing, you can call the IRS business services at 800-829-4933.

In order to open up your corporate bank account, you will need to gather up all of your documents like the articles of incorporation that you received from mycorporation.com and your corporate kit. You will take those with you when you walk into the bank of your choice to open up your corporate bank account.

There is one document/template that you will need very often called a "resolution". The definition of a corporate resolution is, a **corporate** action, sometimes in the form of a legal document, that will be voted on or has been voted on at a meeting of the board of directors for a **corporation**. In layman's terms, it is where you ask the board of directors of your company, which is typically just you, the individual, for permission to do something.

For example, you would have a resolution filled out where the board of directors, which is you, grants permission to open up a bank account, or apply for a line of credit, make a large purchase, etc. It is very simple to do, and you want to keep all your corporate documents, all of your resolutions, and anything related to your business safely filed. These are all internal records for you to keep your corporation organized and professional. These small things go a long way. You need to run your small corporation like a large one.

There are tons of free templates online where you simply fill in the blanks. I will also provide these free forms and fill-in-the-blank templates to you if you subscribe to my website, www.thewealthstrategy.com.

This is the easiest way I can tell you to file your corporation the right way! Easy to follow, step by step, if you have any questions you can always contact us on our website. You can seek a CPA, tax professional, or an attorney. Now that we got the basics out of the way, the next steps are to build the infrastructure of your corporation so that your corporation can become creditable, visible, and fundable.

CHAPTER 7–BUILDING YOUR BUSINESS CREDIBILITY

Congratulations on filing your corporation and getting all the preliminary steps completed. Now you are official. You are no longer an individual, which many entrepreneurs out there are. When you are running around doing business in commerce without a legal entity, you are playing small time. Now you are in the major leagues with the big boys, so we need to take the correct steps to make your corporate entity creditable and fundable so that when you apply for 0% intro-rate credit cards, low-interest-rate lines of credit, private money, and business loans, you get instantly approved without any hassles.

The first thing I recommend doing is a business plan. You want to go through this exercise of writing out all of your business objectives. The best and easiest way I have found to do this, whether you are a beginner or advanced, is by using a fill-in-the-blank program, where it asks you a question section by section of a professional business plan, and all you have to do is fill in the answers for your specific business. This is simple, easy, and less time-consuming, also most importantly, it's free.

There are people and companies out there that will charge you an arm and a leg to write out a professional business plan. Now this business plan is for your own internal records and for your own purposes only. You will not be presenting it to anyone anytime soon so don't worry about making it perfect. The main purpose is that you get familiar with how to put a business plan together and you program your subconscious as you are mapping out each answer for your business plan.

It is a very powerful exercise so make sure you get it done. Google search 'business plan template'; there are a lot of free sites that will allow you to plug in your business info. Follow through each section as it asks you the questions on each section of the business plan. You can organize your ideas by using a service like Mindjet to map out your corporate goals. You will save hundreds of dollars by using a FREE service like Mindjet or a program called bubbl.us.

The next thing I recommend you spend some time doing is cleaning up your personal credit. You want to become a person of integrity who is clean in every aspect of your life. Having a clean personal credit report is very important when it comes to your personal credibility and your business's credibility. You don't necessarily need to have a high credit score, but make sure you don't have anything on your credit that has not been taken care of, like pending collections, open judgments, or any derogatory items that put a blemish on your name.

There are many ways to completely clean up your credit no matter how bad it currently is. You can do it yourself. It is fairly easy with all the free information there is online, but it is very time-consuming. I have a lot of very reputable friends who use credit repair companies that personally guarantee their work or they do not get paid. If you become part of the WealthPreneur Club or join me at www.thewealthstrategy.com, we can help you with some of those connections. We also have free templates and forms to help you with cleaning up your credit and increasing your score. Simply ask through our site.

I hope by now you are starting to realize through reading this book that there are a lot of differences between a normal, average entrepreneur and a WealthPreneur. WealthPreneurs are living their lives with integrity and transparency. Nothing to hide because we do things right. We take care of business. We live balanced lives working each area of our life: family, health, wealth, spirituality.

The next vital step in building your corporation's credibility is creating visibility. You want to let all of the lending institutions, banks, and investors know that you exist and that you are easy to find. The best and fastest way to do that is to sign your business up to all the online and offline business directories, the major local and national 411 phone directories. You will input your business name, phone number, address, etc., all of your corporate information, which makes it easy to locate and get ahold of your business.

Below I will provide some of the directories I suggest you sign up for to obtain max visibility. Make sure you do not pay any of these companies to list you; they always want to upsell you. The free listing they provide works perfectly fine for this exercise. We want to try and save as much as possible when you are a start-up. Here is the list of major directories you want to sign your business up with:

https://www.google.com/mybusiness/

http://www.expressupdate.com/search

http://adsolutions.yp.com/advertise-with-us

https://biz.yelp.com/

http://www.superpages.com/

http://www.citysearch.com

https://www.bingplaces.com/

https://smallbusiness.yahoo.com/local-listings

http://www.localcorporation.com/claim-your-listing/

http://www.listyourself.net/listing.jsp?ID=new

https://signup.citygrid.com

http://my.dexmedia.com//spportal/quickbpflow.do

http://www.dexmedia.com/about/brands/

https://business.yell.com/about-us/

http://www.magicyellow.com/add_your_business.cfm

The next step you want to take in order to make sure your business is visible is to sign up with all the major business catalogs that exist. These catalogs are provided by most of the future lenders you will apply to when you are initially building your business credit. This will be a warm introduction by subscribing to their email list and catalogs online and offline. They will now know you exist before even applying to them for credit. This gives them all of your business information, and they now have it in their database so that you are not a stranger.

Kind of like if you were going to lend money to someone, you would like to know the person a little bit first as opposed to lending money to a complete stranger. That is the same logic with this exercise. Below are the major catalogs you want to subscribe to. All of them are free:

Business Catalogs/Future Lenders

ULINE http://www.uline.com

Seton http://www.seton.com

Quill http://www.quill.com

Reliable http://www.reliable.com

Home Depot http://www.homedepot.com

Lowes http://www.lowes.com

The Great Indoors http://www.thegreatindoors.com

Interstate batteries http://www.interstatebatteries.com

Amazon BUSINESS http://www.amazon.com

Walmart http://www.walmart.com

Sam's Club http://www.samsclub.com

Costco http://www.costco.com

JCPenney http://www.jcpenney.com

Kmart http://www.kmart.com

Gateway http://www.gateway.com

FedEx Office (previously Kinkos) http://fedex.com/us/office

FedEx http://fedex.com

Macys http://www.macys.com

Target http://www.target.com

Sears http://www.sears.com

Myron http://www.myron.com

Discount Filing http://www.discountfiling.com

LSS (Lab Safety Supply) http://www.labsafety.com

Gemplers http://www.gemplers.com

Northern Tool http://www.northerntool.com

Northern Safety http://www.northernsafety.com

HD Supply https://hdsupplysolutions.com

Successories http://www.successories.com

Grainger http://www.grainger.com

CDW http://www.cdw.com

Dell http://www.dell.com

US Plastics http://www.usplastic.com

Rapidforms - Contact for Catalog http://www.rapidforms.com

Franklin Covey http://franklinplanner.com

Gray & Sons http://www.grayandsons.com

Pitney Bowes Virtual Catalog http://www.pb.com

Staples Advantage http://www.staplesadvantage.com

C&H Distributers http://www.chdist.com

Nebs http://www.nebs.com

Staples http://www.staples.com

Office Depot http://www.officedepot.com

Bags & Bows http://www.bagsandbowsonline.com

These are very essential steps to make sure your business has visibility, is verifiable, and will, in turn, become a fundable business. You are creating a free business online account on their website under the business section of their website. This, again, is so that when you go to apply, they have already heard of you and your business info is in their system.

After you have subscribed to all the websites and catalogs and you have listed your business on all local 411 directories online and offline, the next step is to get you a Dun & Bradstreet number and start building your business credit score, which is known as a Paydex score with Dun & Bradstreet and an Intellis score with Experian Business. **It is very important that before you move into the next step that you have verified that your business is listed on 411**. The best and easiest way to check is to dial 411 from your cell phone and ask the automated system or the operator to transfer you to "your business name". If they can locate your business, that is a green light to start the next steps which I will cover in the next chapter to start building your score and obtain as much money as you need to fund your business.

CHAPTER 8–DUN & BRADSTREET, PAYDEX, AND INTELLIS SCORE

I hope that you are extremely excited for this chapter because this is the first chapter where we start talking about how you actually GET THE MONEY! We have been talking about a lot of important, mindset stuff, business structure, and credibility. Now finally we will get into what some people are all about, which is the money. How do I get money, Ruddy?

Now that your business is verifiable, you are on 411, you have all the visibility tools set up for your corporation, it is time for you and your business to meet Dun & Bradstreet aka "D&B". It always amazes me how so many business owners who have been in business for quite some time have never heard of D&B. They are the world's largest credit reporting agency. They report companies worldwide. They are the mafia for credit reporting. You definitely want to be on their good side. In this chapter I will show you some ninja tricks on how to do just that.

Here is a little history on D&B:

Dun & Bradstreet, Inc. is an American public company that provides commercial data to businesses on credit history, business-to-business sales and marketing, counterparty risk exposure, supply chain management, lead scoring, and social identity matching.

The company's database contains information on more than 235 million companies across 200 countries worldwide. Dun & Bradstreet has been listed on the Fortune 500 and was one of the first companies to be publicly traded on the New York Stock Exchange.

Dun & Bradstreet was started on July 20, 1841, with the formation of the Mercantile Agency in New York City by Lewis Tappan, later called R.G. Dun & Company. He recognized the need for a centralized credit reporting system. Tappan formed the company to create a network of correspondents who would provide reliable, objective credit information to subscribers.

As an advocate for civil rights, Tappan used his abolitionist connections to expand and update the company's credit information. In spite of accusations for invading personal privacy, by 1844 the Mercantile Agency had over 280 clients. The agency continued to expand across international boundaries.

In 1933, Dun merged with competitor, John M. Bradstreet to form today's Dun & Bradstreet. The Data Universal Numbering System (DUNS) was invented in 1962.

What you need to do next is get your "DUNS NUMBER". This is the number that D&B will use to identify your business. The DUNS number will allow you to build a Paydex score. **Paydex** is a term used in business for a numerical business score for the promptness of your payments to the creditors. The Paydex score is used for commercial organizations in a manner similar to the way the FICO score is used for individuals.

Paydex is calculated based on one single factor. The factor is contingent upon whether the business makes their payments either "as agreed" or "better than agreed".

The Paydex score ranges from 0 to 100 (best). A Paydex of 80 or higher is considered healthy for a company - that is, a company is paying its suppliers and vendors on time and before the scheduled payment due date. It is also important to note that payments received after they are due, meaning late, will negatively affect the organization's Paydex score. Today, most lenders and suppliers are looking for a score of 80 and higher.

That will be our immediate goal after getting our DUNS Number, to get to an 80 Paydex score. I am going to teach you how to do that very quickly. But first, let's take a step back and talk about getting your DUNS number.

In order to get your DUNS number, Dun & Bradstreet typically will sell you a business builder package ranging between $500-$700 USD that includes your DUNS number. You will not be requesting your D&B Number on their website because we are trying to save as much money as possible as a start-up at this point.

The secret to this part of the process is the following: There is a secret VIP way around it, instead of going directly through Dun & Bradstreet. Dun & Bradstreet has an area for government contractors or future government contractors.

The website is called www.iupdate.dnb.com. This is a new version of the Central Contractors' Registry. The new portal is called **S**ystem for **A**ward **M**anagement. The SAM database will prepare your business to sell to the U.S. government along with giving you the ability to participate in government contracting, etc. Not that you need to, but this will allow your business the ability to, if it ever wanted. It also looks extremely reputable for your corporation.

Going through SAM will get you listed as a preferred business vendor that's positioned to sell to the government and or bid on government contracts. They will assign you a **CAGE CODE** number for your business. It's just another file locator number to verify your identity and to prove that you've been vetted.

Before they allow you to fill out your profile on SAM, you will be required to get a DUNS number to initiate the registration process. That is exactly our objective in doing this step.

You accomplish two things: You start your profile on SAM, but you also enter the Dun & Bradstreet application process through the VIP line so that they view you as a potential government contractor and not some average person who will be another sales lead to them to sell your business reports, credit builder packages, and so forth. Also this allows your business to get your DUNS number free of charge! Cha-Ching!

When you go into www.iupdate.dnb.com, you will be clicking on "Request a DUNS number." You will then fill out an application. Make sure you have the following items ready:

Corporate legal name, physical address, telephone number that's in 411, contact name, SIC, and NAICS Code (line of business). They will ask questions like, number of employees at your location? Do you have a parent corporate entity? Is this a home-based business? Etc. Simple questions that you provide simple answers to.

After you submit all the requested information, Dun & Bradstreet will email you within a week with your DUNS number. Congratulations on getting your DUNS number!

When you're issued a DUNS number through SAM/iupdate... Dun & Bradstreet puts you in a different category and takes you seriously, just like a large corporation. They assume that you actually know what you're doing.

Let's talk about SAM and how it can potentially benefit you and your corporation. The System for Award Management (SAM) is combining federal procurement systems and the Catalog of Federal Domestic Assistance into one new system that allows you to bid on government contracts.

Who is Required to Register in the SAM & CCR?

Since October 2003, it is federally mandated that any organization wishing to do business with the federal government under a Federal Acquisition Regulation Contract or FAR-based Contract, must be registered in CCR before being awarded a contract.

I'd rather you HAVE the ability to do business with the government and NEVER use it than have an opportunity to fulfill a huge contract and you NOT knowing what to do next.

The government, unfortunately, always overpays for the contracts they outsource. They may pay $1 million for repaving some streets when the real cost is 700k.

If your business is registered with SAM, you are able to bid on the contract even though you don't pave streets. You can always outsource it to someone who can fulfill the contract and you just get paid a portion of the contract.

How Much Does it Cost to Get Listed in the CCR through SAM? Nothing, because it's a federally funded program. There is no cost to get listed.

How Can this SAM Process Help Me?

The government is into diversity and helping everyone out on a level playing field. Sometimes contract jobs are awarded specifically to women-operated and -owned businesses.

If you fall under one of the following categories, you may get priority in an "RFB" request for bids. Do any of the following apply to you? Self-Certified Small Disadvantaged Business, Service-Disabled Veteran-Owned, Non-Profit Agency, Veteran-Owned Business, Woman-Owned Business, Minority-Owned business?

When you register with the SAM/CCR, you automatically have a chance to sell your product or service to many government institutions as a pre-approved vendor.

They only want to speak with true business people who are performers and ready to supply. SAM prescreens tire kickers and others who may not "seriously" be in business.

The number that you'll get from the SAM is called a CAGE number or CAGE code. The Commercial and Government Entity (CAGE) Code is a five-character ID number used extensively within the federal government. You can obtain a CAGE Code for your corporation by following these steps.

1. Make sure you now have a DUNS Number.

2. Go to the System for Award Management website which is https://www.sam.gov/portal/SAM and look for the link that says, "Create User Account." It's generally a quick link on the left-hand side.

3. Next look for the link that says "Register/Update Entity." Now you may start the registration process to get a CAGE Code.

4. If you run into any questions and need immediate assistance, contact me on my website www.thewealthstrategy.com

If you are a beginner, all this information may be a tad bit overwhelming, but I promise if you take it step by step, it is very easy. If you get stuck, simply seek help. You know how to get a hold of me or someone in my team.

Now that you have a DUNS number and a CAGE code, you should put this somewhere very visible in the footer of your website. The footer of your website should read something like this

DUNS#   07111111 | NAICS   Code:541611 | CAGE Code:7C000 | Corp Name Inc. © 2015 | All Rights Reserved.

CHAPTER 9-UNLIMITED FUNDING FOR YOUR IDEAS AND VISION

Okay, finally! We can start building your Paydex score and your Intellis score by strategically applying for business credit, to the right creditors that we know for sure will approve your business for credit and funding.

The strategy will be to apply to the right lenders in the right order to get your Paydex score above 80. First you build your Paydex score, which is with D&B, and then you build your Intellis score which is with Experian Business.

We will be applying to the lenders in four different phases.

Phase1- We will start with **Phase One** vendors, which will be the lenders that are the easiest to get approved for. These lenders are called "Net 30 credit" vendors, which means you apply for credit with them, but anything you borrow you must pay in full within thirty days. This is great because that means that they will be reporting anything you borrow and pay fairly quickly. The trick is to initially apply to three of these types of vendors at the same time.

You borrow anywhere from $100-$300 USD in the form of buying something from their online store on Net 30 terms. Then you wait and pay the accounts in full on the day the bill is due.

It usually takes about fifteen days from the day you pay them for them to report to Dun & Bradstreet. So you are looking at about a forty-five-day cycle before those first three lenders report your "on-time payment" to D&B.

After those first three lenders report your on-time-payment, it is time to apply to three more Net 30-type vendors, who will also report your punctual payment to D&B, making it a total of six creditors for Phase 1 that will report your on-time payments to your D&B report.

The first three magical lenders that will approve you and report your payments are:

1. Quill www.Quill.com
2. Grainger www.Grainger.com.
3. Uline www.uline.com

(*VERY IMPORTANT side note for Grainger and Uline: You will need to buy somethingfrom them online, any item ranging from $10-$20, before applying for a Net 30 account, so that the purchase can auto generate your account number with them.)

The following three lenders for Phase 1 are:

4. HD Supply www.hdsupplysolutions.com
5. Office Depo www.officedepo.com
6. Fedex www.fedex.com/us/office

So to recap on Phase 1, you apply to the first three lenders, pay the accounts on the day they are due, wait fifteen days after your payment, and apply to the following three lenders. The nice thing is if you notice these lenders you are applying to are the same ones you should have already subscribed to on their respective websites and online catalogs if you followed previous steps.

For the next phase you will need to wait another fifteen days from date of payments. You also want to make sure all the lenders from Phase 1 have reported the payments on to your business credit report.

Phase 2- The second phase of lenders will be some Net 30 and some open credit accounts. You will be using a similar method as before where you apply for three different lenders at the same time or the same day. The first three for Phase 2 are:

1. Amazon Business www.amazon.com/gp/cobrandcard (you will be applying for their Business Line of Credit.)
2. Global Secured Card www.csiglobalvcard.com
3. Global Fleet https://www.global-fleet.com/apply-now/

Same thing as before. You will utilize about $100-$200 from the available credit on each card then pay it in full and wait the fifteen days until your payments have been reported to the business credit bureaus.

At this point you should have about nine lenders reporting on your report with on-time payments. The next lenders for Phase 2 are:

4. https://www.capitalone.com/credit-cards/business/spark-cash Capital One Spark Cash (0% intro period)
5. Home Depo https://www.citicards.com/cards/HOMEDEPOT

You will use a few hundred on those two accounts as well, then pay them in full and on time, then wait the forty-five days for your on-time payment reports to the business bureaus.

As you can see, with this strategy you now have eleven lenders that trust your business and are reporting that your business is trustworthy and makes their payments on time. By this point you can rest assured that your Paydex score is at a minimum of 80.

If you look at the time frame, there were forty-five-plus days from the initial three from Phase 1, another forty-five-plus days for the second part of Phase 1, forty-five-plus days from Phase 2 part 1, and another forty-five days from part 2 of Phase 2.

So this is about 180 days, which is six months, to build a solid Paydex score and reputable Dun & Bradstreet report. At this point, your business will start getting flooded with offers via mail from all kinds of lenders and financial institutions wanting to give your business money, loans, and funding. You do not want to take any offers with high interest.

Phase 3 is where you really start seeing the money that you can use to grow your business and fund your dreams and ideas.

This phase will also start building your Intellis score, which is the Experian Business report so that your business is very low risk to any lender, investor, or bank looking to lend you money or invest in your business.

For Phase 3 you will be applying for credit to powerful financial institutions that can lend you a substantial amount of money. You want to make sure all of the other eleven lenders from Phases 1 and 2 have reported your on-time payments for at least two months each. You will apply to the following:

1. Discover Business (You must call them over the phone to open up a business credit card or line of credit. Always ask for their 0% intro period).
2. Chase Ink www.chase.com/prequalified
3. American Express Business Simply Cash www.americanexpress.com

Between these three accounts alone, you should be able to obtain about 40-50k in funding at 0% interest for nine to twelve months. A few things you want to do with each of these accounts is:

A. You want to make sure you choose the option that has an intro period of 0%.

B. You want to make sure that when you get approved, you call them before activating the cards and ask them for an increase on the available line of credit. Tell them you want to use the card as your primary spend card and your business needs more available credit. I would ask them to double the amount they approved you for. They may or may not do it, but you don't know unless you ask.

C. Call them every three to six months to ask for an increase on the available line of credit.

After you have had these accounts for about three to six months, if you need more financing you can apply to:

4. Bank Of American Platinum www.business.bankofamerica.com

5. U.S. Bank Business Edge Platinum www.usbank.com/small-business (0% for 12months)

You would also do the above steps A-C for these accounts and any other accounts in the future.

Guys, at this point you should have roughly sixteen lenders reporting on your Dun & Bradstreet and about half of these also reporting on Experian Business report making your Intellis score above 80 as well, which is considered a very low-risk business.

You should be proud of yourself and the reputable business you are creating. You are building a strong foundation and have access to money so that you can fund any idea or investment you want. You want to make sure you are strategic about what you start using this money on. You need to make sure anything you use this money on will give you a great return on investment.

For example, you buy a product to sell for 1,000 USD and you can sell it quickly for 3,000 USD; there are a lot of opportunities like that out there once you have money in hand.

You want to make sure if you do not know what to do with the money, seek help. Get a reputable business coach like myself or someone you trust who can help you strategize how to make the best use out of this money.

If you are not 100% confident on what you are investing the money in, don't! This is a big responsibility. You do not want to spend the money you have available of frivolous things. You need to make sure any money you borrow at a 0% or low interest, you can pay back, and not only pay it back but make a profit from it, also known as a spread and arbitrage.

I will talk more about how you can invest your money in the last part of this book. But I wanted to make sure I warned you just in case you only read this far and don't finish this book because you're too busy spending the money and getting yourself in trouble not being able to pay it back.

Okay, let's go over the last phase of building your business credit and acquiring money from lenders and financial institutions. Phase 4 is where you now have excellent business credit, you have been responsible with all the sixteen lenders that are reporting your business to the business credit bureaus. You are using the funding wisely and are making some money from the money that you borrowed. You have seasoned your business for over twelve months now.

It is time to start living the corporate lifestyle to the fullest and make sure everything is under your corporation's name. Your cell phones, any lease agreements, anything where you are required to make a payment should no longer be in your personal name. It is under the business name.

You now can apply for a car loan or preferably a car lease under the business name. You can apply at Ford Motor Credit or Mercedes-Benz, whatever you like. Most car companies will approve your business for fleet vehicles for which approvals can range as low as 250k and above. Although you may only need a $20-30 thousand vehicle, the line of credit is there in case you need more company cars in the future.

You can also start applying for business lines of credit with all the major financial institutions like Wells Fargo, Citibank, Chase, and Bank of America. You can also try private lenders like my friends at Aurelian Commercial Lending www.AurelianLending.com where they can approve your business for commercial lines of credit of 100k plus (their main criteria for approving loans is credit worthiness) which you can use for real estate or any investment you want.

Having a solid business credit report that shows your business entity is trustworthy can get you money from private investors as well. Big investors will check your D&B and Experian Business report, but most importantly with private investors, they want to make sure they like you and that you, the individual, is savvy, trustworthy, and competent enough to make them a profit from the money they invest with you.

Private Investors

Private investors are very different than banks, private lenders, and lending institutions. Private investors are usually wealthy individuals, a small group of individuals that have a substantial amount of money and they are looking for talented entrepreneurs to invest their money with. The technical definition is an affluent individual who provides capital for a business start-up, usually in exchange for convertible debt or ownership equity. A small but increasing number of investors organize themselves into angel groups or angel networks to share research and pool their investment capital, as well as to provide advice to their portfolio companies.

Private investors are not looking for just any newbie, rookie entrepreneur; they are looking for someone like a WealthPreneur, which I am grooming you to become through this book. They invest in people and business that they feel logically and emotionally will give them a great rate of return on their investment. When dealing with a private investor, the business report is just an icing on the cake. If they don't trust you and your ability to perform, they won't invest their money no matter how great your corporate scores are!

Private investors invest in all types of business ideas like real estate projects, entertainment, contracting, construction, brokerage, loans, catering, retail, photography, consulting practices, beauty and health products, interior design, online businesses, education-based business, and many others. Private investors tend to invest based on goals, interests, and location.

Investments from private investors are estimated at approximately $130 to $150 billion of private money annually.

Most private investors tend to invest in businesses located within forty miles or so of their homes or offices, something about keeping things close. Although now with modern technology, investors feel more comfortable investing further out since video phone conversations are more common and the Internet makes you feel like distances are shrinking and the world seems smaller and definitely more connected.

Some common reasons why private investors reject a deal are lack of growth potential, overpriced equity, under-qualified or untalented management, or lack of information and trust with the entrepreneur. The one main point you need to get across to your investor is, what is in it for them? How safe is their return on investment, and why should they invest their money with you over anyone else? If those points are clear, your chances of them investing with you are very likely.

Finding private investors has become much easier with modern communication mediums like the Internet and investor search program. There are now tons of websites that give you lists of private investors and outline their profiles of what they are interested in investing in and the terms they prefer.

The best way to find a private investor in my opinion is networking in social clubs, investor meet-ups that you can find on www.meetup.com . Personal relationships and introductions are a great way to start a business relationship or partnership with an investor. Ask your friends, family, and mentors for introductions. If you don't currently have mentors, look for well-known people in your community. These mentors could be entrepreneurs in your industry who have successfully raised capital before. If you cannot find a private investor through personal networking, then you can always go online to the types of sites I mentioned earlier.

Here are some popular websites to meet investors and pique their interest to meet with you for an actual pitch or your business venture:

www.investorscircle.net

www.techcoastangels.com

www.newyorkangels.com

www.allianceofangels.com

www.hydeparkangels.com

www.ohiotechangels.com/

www.fundingpost.com

www.searching4privateinestors.com

www.angelcapitalassociation.org

www.contactprivateinvestors.com

Some advantages of working with private investors are that they typically have an area of expertise in the kinds of projects they fund, and they don't fund projects they don't see a need for or personally believe in. If you can successfully pitch an investor, you can rest assured that you can sell because they are one of the world's toughest and most demanding individuals. I have sat down with many investors, and one thing that has always worked is that I am very transparent. All my investors have always told me that after my pitches, "Ruddy, I love that you are very transparent." I will teach you my persuasion and effective pitch techniques in part 4 of this book. It is all in order for a reason.

Wise investors will many times step in and offer you counsel. Most of the time this advice is well worth considering. I have had more than one investor open doors, make introductions, and provide entrees to new clients and opportunities that have been priceless.

Whether you are raising capital through your business credit using financial institutions or private investors, you need to be presenting yourself as a professional, knowledgeable, and well-versed corporation. When doing business, you are conducting yourself like a business and in the way large corporations present themselves in commerce.

This is the corporate lifestyle where you personally own nothing but control everything, which is a line from Nelson Rockefeller. You don't own it; the corporation does, but you control the corporation. Like it or not, these are the rules we live by in the modern world so learn how they work, and take advantage of them in an ethical way.

.

CHAPTER 10–CROWDFUNDING AND KICKSTARTER

I hope up to this point, I have been able to transfer a wealth of knowledge to you about raising capital and obtaining funding. I taught you a powerful strategy to structure your business's foundation so that you can position your business to use business credit to obtain as much money as you want from lenders, creditors, and financial institutions, and even private investors. Now I am going to teach you how to raise capital from normal everyday people using the power of the Internet. This is a revolutionary new way to fund any idea, any dream, any project that you have. The concept is called "Crowdfunding". This is a concept that didn't exist twenty years ago and has really gotten popular in the last five or so years.

Thanks to the Internet, you now have the power to share your idea, your project, your business, your dreams with people all around the world, and through crowd funding you can have thousands of people each pay a small portion to fund your project.

Crowdfunding gives you the power to bring entire businesses to life overnight. But what is crowdfunding exactly? How can you use it to provide venture capital for any project or start-up? I will go over how you as a WealthPreneur, can utilize it to create your own successful crowdfunding campaign. There has been millions of dollars raised just in the last twelve months in crowdfunding campaigns, with success stories like Wasteland 2 who raised over $3 million on one project from normal everyday people. These numbers are only increasing. This is great news for inventors, entrepreneurs, and start-ups. The power of numbers of thousands of people investing/donating a little bit of money each can quickly turn into a significant amount of money.

The key to a strong campaign is that you clearly convey your vision to potential backers, and you use powerful language as well as video to engage with your audience and have people buy in to your project. It is to collectively bring together the general public to see what you are envisioning.

Using crowdfunding, anyone can make their idea a reality. It is now possible for normal everyday people to launch nearly any promising start-up project or business as long as there is real passion behind what you are presenting to the general public.

Let's get started. Crowdfunding is simply the process of asking the general public for donations that provide start-up capital for new ventures. Using this strategy, entrepreneurs and small-business owners can bypass banks, financial institutions, lenders, venture capitalists, and angel investors entirely and instead pitch ideas straight to everyday online Internet users, who provide financial backing.

Another powerful advantage is that it allows you to see if there is even a market for your idea. If none is willing to pay for it or donate anything to see it come alive, then it may not make sense to make it or start it. If you get any decent amount of people wanting to donate into the project, then it is validation that you have something worth bringing to market.

The best crowdfunding services, in my opinion, are Kickstarter.com and IndieGogo.com. They are the top websites where you can create a project for the general public to see and donate towards. They host the information, photos, and promotional videos on products, projects, or services that are looking to get funded.

These websites have millions of viewers whom you can offer your idea or business venture to. You offer special rewards in exchange for pledges that support your project, rather than equity or a share of the profits. The benefits that the people who donate into your project receive are exclusive merchandise, advance access to new releases, or more personal incentives.

Let's say you wanted to write a book, and you had a great concept for it so you started a campaign to raise 50k to write and publish the book. You would say, for example, anyone donating $15 towards the 50k will get a signed copy of the book; $40 will get a signed book and audio book; and a $600 donation will receive private consultation on what the book entails. For a larger donation (say, $1500), you might get a personal invite to an exclusive launch party and one-one mentorship etc. People can donate whatever they can afford. No matter what your idea is, you can test it on there for free to see if it will get funded.

There are 7.1 billion people on the planet and about two billion people on the Internet 24/7/365 every second of every day. All you need to do is get a tiny fraction of those people to see your vision and share your passion. That's what's so fascinating about the scale of the

Internet and using crowdfunding. If you simply got just 2,500 out of millions of users on Kickstarter.com to donate/invest an average of just $20 each, that will get you to 50k. There are a lot of people raising six figures in thirty days or less on this platform.

The phenomenal thing about crowdfunding is that you are testing ideas for free, you risk very little, and can have huge gain because you have the potential to receive all the financing you are asking for to start a product, service, business, or invention. The best part is that you find the customers willing to pay for it before you even make it, so you have a client base that supports you and is likely to buy future products, so you have clientele base, a market base before you even go into business. In my opinion this is one of the best things that has happened to modern-day business since the Internet.

Another significant advantage of crowdfunding is that you don't give away any ownership or equity stake in your business like you typically would with a private investor. Traditional sources of investment typically require that you give up a portion of a company or project in exchange for their support, or that you pay back the investment with interest. Also when you have investors you need to satisfy, there is a lot of pressure since they expect a quick return on investment.

I will go over some quick pros and cons about crowdfunding since I know some of you are thinking this is too good to be true. I will start with the pros. Aside from all the awesome things I have already discussed, here are some additional pros.

Pros:

1. An added benefit of crowdfunding campaigns is that you will often receive useful advice – and even true offers of assistance – from backers who want you to succeed and will do everything they can to help you get there. They become your alliance marketing team that help to promote your project to all their friends and family.

2. You keep all the profits and equity: Projects and businesses remain 100% yours.

3. You are preselling your product or service, which means you may be able to get more than the actual retail value from backers who believe in your project. Also you are risk mitigating and earning capital that can be directly applied towards production and marketing costs at the same time.

4. You have full 100% control over the entire project, costs, timing, delivery, vision and execution, marketing and customer interactions.

Cons:

1. You are putting your ideas and passion in front of the general public who will be scrutinizing it and judging what you believe in. Sometimes the feedback can be harsh so don't take it personally. There are a lot of haters out there who want to bring you down. Also you are exposing your ideas to competitors who may see it as a great idea and copy it themselves. These are risks you take in most businesses though.

2. You will need to invest a lot of time and effort into social marketing campaigns and constant self-promotion throughout the entire duration of the fundraising campaign. If you're shy,

scared, and do not like to sell, you either need to get over those fears or just save your time and go a different route because this may not be a good one for you. In order to have a successful crowdfunding campaign, you or someone you trust needs to become a 24/7 project spokesman and strong ethical salesperson.

3. Crowdfunding requires that you do your research on something called message-to-market match. This means you have something that interests a significant amount of people strongly enough to motivate them to part with their money. The research needs to be precise, and making a mistake can mean doing a lot of work with little to no results. When running a crowdfunding campaign, success is not guaranteed. You may fail like in anything else and not get any funding for the campaign in which you invested a lot of time and effort.

Crowdfunding is not for everyone, but if you have a strong message-to-market match, it is a phenomenal way to raise capital and fund your idea, project, and future businesses. The first campaign will be the toughest. Once you get the gist of how it all works, you can launch as many campaigns as you want.

I will now take you by the hand and walk you through how you can launch a crowdfunding campaign.

The first thing you need to do is pick a crowdfunding platform. My favorite is www.kickstarter.com because I am not very good with technology, and their platform is very user-friendly. In 2014, 22,252 creative projects were successfully funded on Kickstarter. $529 million was pledged to Kickstarter projects in 2014. That's more than $1,000 a minute. Kickstarter is open to any kind of project, and it is now worldwide. Approval is required to launch a campaign. Kickstarter provides many levels of support from the time you begin developing your campaign until after it is completed.

Their platform allows easy integration into social media and individual websites. Every platform charges a fee for providing the crowdfunding platform service. For Kickstarter the fees are 5% of your intended goal and you only pay if you meet the goal. Processing fees vary from 3-5% via Amazon. For the funding goal, you must reach the goal or get nothing, which is why it is important that you set an attainable goal. If you surpass your goal, you get every donation above your intended goal, but you still will pay the 5% fee to Kickstarter from the total funding.

There are many other platforms that you can pick, like www.Indiegogo.com, www.rockethub.com www.crowdcube.com or www.growvc.com. You can check each one out and see which one resonates with you the most and simply pick one for your crowdfunding campaign.

The second thing you want to do is spend time doing research for the type of project that you are thinking of launching. The market research should be the following:

1. Am I offering something that a significant amount of everyday online users are interested in?
2. Is the project you are launching something you are so passionate about that others will jump on board and part with their money?
3. What makes what you are offering different and unique?

4. Who is your target audience? How is your project going to impact your audience?

5. What is your one-minute elevator pitch for your project? Is the one-minute pitch compelling enough that if you heard it you would buy?

6. What approach or angel will you take for your project? Will it be serious? Professional? Humorous? Short and to the point? Touching story? Informative? Etc.

Make sure you have a genre that you stick to. One that I have found is very powerful in today's age is humor. If you can convey a message with good content and it can make a large group of people laugh, then that is what I call disruptive marketing. We will talk more about marketing in part three of this book.

7. What is your call to action? What exactly do you want from the audience/backers? Make sure it is very specific and clear.

8. Make sure you create a powerful video for your project that tells your story and gives the audience a strong visual of what you are looking to accomplish.

9. Is your video is a well-structured ethical sales pitch? I will teach you the best sales techniques in part four of this book in case you are not good at sales. Sales skill is the key to any successful venture.

10. Make sure the video includes your contact information on how the audience can get in touch with you and your project because you will be posting this video on websites, social media, and most importantly, having other people sharing the video on their social media and social platforms.

You need to do your research on all ten of those items. The next thing you need to do is figure out what kind of rewards you will be gifting your backers with. You need to have a motivating reward to give to every person who invest/donates money to your campaign. Be very strategic and put some thought into what you will be gifting people in exchange for their donation.

A few things to consider when coming up with the rewards you will provide your backers:

1. Would you pay the amount of money you are requesting people to donate for what you are offering?

2. Make sure you have different levels of donations. The more someone donates, the more they should receive. Have anywhere from three to five different levels of potential donations, but make sure each level up is more and more enticing for your audience.

3. Will you provide physical merchandise or virtual? For example, you can provide a book or an eBook. You can provide a physical DVD or a downloadable file, etc. Choose whatever you feel most comfortable with.

4. Do some research on previous projects that were successful in raising their intended funding goal projects that are similar in genre to the project you are launching. The research is to get ideas on what kind of rewards worked best since your audience will be similar to theirs. You can do some of this research on the platforms we discussed earlier like www.kickstarter.com .

The next step that is extremely important is determining a funding goal. How much do you need to raise? This is crucial because remember, with Kickstarter.com, if you don't reach your goal, all of the money goes back to the people who donated if you don't reach your goal. So be sure to do you research before coming up with a number.

For your first campaign, I suggest a small amount, 20k-50k, depending on the project. That way you get the mechanics on how it works, you build fans/backers for your project who may donate for later and bigger projects. Here are some things to consider when creating a funding goal:

1. Look into projects in your field that failed. Why did they fail? Learn what not to do.
2. Look into projects that succeeded in your field. What funding ranges seem to be most successful? Why? Learn what they did.
3. Consider the size of target audience vs. funding goal set.
4. How was the community involved, and how did fans respond to the successful projects as well as those projects who failed?

That last question leads us into the next part of launching your campaign.

The last thing that you need to determine when launching your crowdfunding campaign is, how you are going to market the campaign? This is the part that can potentially cost you some money. The nice thing is if you are following this book in the correct order, the previous chapters teach you how to raise lines of credit and credit cards at 0% interest, which is money that you can use for marketing anything, including a crowdfunding campaign.

If you have a huge following and have thousands of friends on social media like Facebook, Twitter, Instagram, a personal website or blog, etc. or maybe you belong to a large church or social interactive groups like a real estate club, then marketing your crowdfunding campaign can be free just by word-of-mouth and having your friends share to their social media groups.

If you don't have thousands of contacts with people online and offline, then you will need to spend a little bit of money on marketing primarily online, which is basically just spreading the word about the project campaign you are launching or have launched. I will be giving you very powerful information on how to market anything online and offline in the next part of this book.

But as far as crowdfunding goes for marketing your campaign, follow similar steps as before. Look at what others in your field have found the most effective for marketing their campaigns. Here are some easy marketing tips to consider:

1. Infiltrate your own personal network of friends and family. Make sure they help to share your campaign with their whole network of friends and family.
2. Reach out to influential people in your field who have a huge following and see if they will help promote your campaign. (You can reach a lot of these people by Facebook messenger or LinkedIn. Message as many as you can, even if one or two agree to help, that can be a huge help and a big reach to thousands of people in your field.)

3. Use pay-per-click ads on Facebook, Twitter, or YouTube. (I'll teach you effective ways to do this in later chapters if you don't already know how.)

4. Contact websites in your field that have a huge following and millions of visitors and see how much it will cost you to advertise your campaign with them.

5. Contact online publications like Huffington Post, LA Times, etc. and see if you can connect with someone who will write an article or publication on the campaign you are passionately launching. (This is why you must be absolutely passionate about what you are doing because only if you are passionate will you be able to move others to take action on helping you with your dream.)

So to wrap up on this fascinating modern-day concept of crowdfunding, here is a little recap of the fundamental things you will need to run a powerful and successful campaign.

1. You will need a strong desire to succeed and be 100% passionate on selling the vision for your idea, product, or dream business.

2. You will need to do your research before you start. If you fail to plan, you plan to fail.

3. A strong video that sells your project clearly and concisely. Make sure it has strong professional imagery and language.

4. You have compelling gifts and rewards that move people to action so that your audience donates at a high volume and quantity.

5. A solid platform that allows you to stay in touch and constant communication with your fans/backers.

6. Effective marketing that promotes sharing of your campaign through social media and any and all online platforms. Viral marketing campaigns using as much video as possible. Video marketing is very effective in today's age.

7. You will need to create a trustworthy brand for your project, preferably you, but can be someone you trust who will be the face behind the project. Make sure that person proudly and ethically represents the brand and, most importantly, transfers the level of passion for the project that you can utilize as an advocate.

There you have it, WealthPreneurs. The last chapter of positioning yourself to raise capital. You have no excuse in today's modern day and age to not accomplish your dreams. All the money in the world you need is available if you are truly passionate and willing to put in the work.

Now that you know specific, actionable strategies on how to get the money and raise unlimited capital, it is time to talk about how you promote your business, your ideas, your brand, your services, truly anything you want to promote online and offline -- effective marketing techniques that work in today's age.

Part 3 **Promote**, part 4 **Persuade** and part 5
Prosper will continue on BOOK 2 which will be
chapters 11-23...

Please write an honest review of this book online.

FIVE-STAR RATING!

Thank You,

www.ingramcontent.com/pod-product-compliance
Lightning Source LLC
Chambersburg PA
CBHW081154180526
45170CB00006B/2083